$4 —

SA

MW01065434

Pascale Couture

ULYSSES
TRAVEL PUBLICATIONS
Travel better... enjoy more

Series Director Claude Morneau	*Editing* Tracy Kendrick	*Collaboration* Benoit Prieur
Research and *Composition* Pascale Couture	*Layout* Jennifer McMorran	*Graphic Design* Jean-François Bienvenue
Cartography André Duchesne	*Artistic Director* Patrick Farei Atoll Direction	*Photography* Pascale Couture *Photo headings* Jennifer McMorran
English Translation Jennifer McMorran	*Illustrations* Marie-Anik Viatour	

We would also like to thank: Constance Haward (Signature Vacations); the staff at the Office du Tourisme de Saint-Barthélemy.

Distributors

AUSTRALIA:
Little Hills Press
11/37-43 Alexander St.
Crows Nest NSW 2065
☎ (612) 437-6995
Fax: (612) 438-5762

GREAT BRITAIN:
World Leisure Marketing
9 Downing Road West
Meadows, Derby
UK DE21 6HA
☎ 1 332 343 332
Fax: 1 332 340 464

SPAIN:
Altaïr
Balmes 69
E-08007 Barcelona
☎ (34-3) 323-3062
Fax: (3403) 451-2559

CANADA:
Ulysses Books & Maps
4176 Saint-Denis
Montréal, Québec
H2W 2M5
☎ (514) 843-9882, ext.
Fax: 514-843-9448

ITALY:
Edizioni del Riccio
50143 Firenze-
Via di Soffiano
☎ (055) 71 63 50
Fax: (055) 71 33 33

U.S.A.:
Seven Hills Book Distributors
49 Central Avenue
Cincinnati, Ohio, 45202
☎ 1-800-545-2005
Fax: (513) 381-0753

GERMANY & AUSTRIA:
Brettschneider Fernreisebedarf
GmbH
85586 Poing bei München
Hauptstr. 5
☎ 08121-71436
Fax: 08121-71419

NETHERLANDS and FLANDERS:
Nilsson & Lamm
Pampuslaan 212-214
Postbus 195
1380 AD Weesp (NL)
☎ 02940-65044
Fax: 02940-15054

Other countries, contact Ulysses Books & Maps (Montréal), Fax : (514) 843-9448

Canadian Cataloguing in Publication Data

Pascale Couture 1966-

    Saint Barts

    (Ulysses Due South)
    Includes index.
    Translation of Saint-Barthélemy

ISBN 2-89464-002-1

1. Saint-Barthélemy - Guidebooks. I. Title. II. Series

F2089.C6813 1995   917.297'6   C95-941430-4

A wonderful bird is a pelican,
His bill will hold more than his belican.
He can take in his beak
Food enough for a week,
But I'm damned if I see how the helican.

The Pelican
Dixon Lanier Merritt

TABLE OF CONTENTS

Help make Ulysses Travel Guides even better!

The information contained in this guide was correct at press time. However, mistakes can slip in, omissions are always possible, places can disappear, etc. The author and publisher hereby disclaim any liability for loss or damage resulting from omissions or errors.

We value your comments, corrections and suggestions, as they allow us to keep each guide up to date. The best contributions will be rewarded with a free book from Ulysses Travel Publications. All you have to do is write us at the following address and indicate which title you would be interested in receiving (see the list at end of guide).

Ulysses Travel Publications
4176 Rue Saint-Denis
Montréal, Québec
Canada H2W 2M5

LIST OF MAPS

TABLE OF SYMBOLS

☎	Telephone number
⇄	Fax number
≡	Air conditioning
⊗	Ceiling fan
≈	Pool
ℜ	Restaurant
⊛	Whirlpool
ℝ	Refrigerator
ℂ	Kitchenette
tv	Colour television
pb	Private bath
bkfst	Breakfast

ATTRACTION CLASSIFICATION

★	Interesting
★★	Worth a visit
★★★	Not to be missed

HOTEL CLASSIFICATION

Unless otherwise indicated, accommodation prices are for one room, double occupancy, during the high season.

RESTAURANT CLASSIFICATION

The prices in the guide are for a meal for two people, including tip, but exluding drinks.

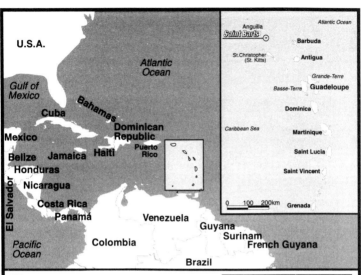

Where is Saint Barts?

The Island of Saint Barts

Overseas French department
Main City: Gustavia
Language: French
Population: 5,000 inhab.
Currency: French franc
Area: 25 km²

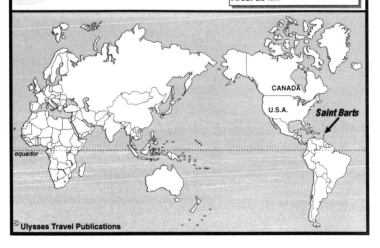

© Ulysses Travel Publications

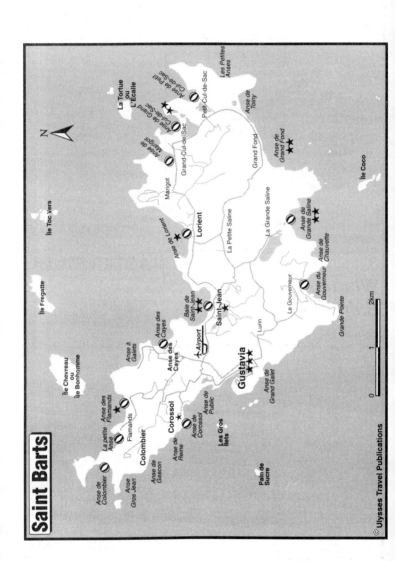

Saint Barts

N

Île Toc Vers

Île Fregatte

Île Chevreau ou Île Bonhomme

Anse de Colombier

La petite Anse

Anse des Flamands

Colombier

Flamands

Anse de Gascon

Anse de Reine

Anse de Corossol

Corossol

Les Gros Îlets

Anse de Public

Anse à Galets

Anse des Cayes

Anse des Cayes

Airport

Baie de Saint-Jean

Saint-Jean

Lurin

Gustavia

Anse de Grand Galet

Pain de Sucre

Grande Pointe

Le Gouverneur

Anse du Gouverneur

Anse de Chauvette

La Grande Saline

Anse de Grande Saline

La Petite Saline

Lorient

Anse de Lorient

Marigot

Anse de Marigot

Anse de Grand Cul-de-Sac

La Tortue ou L'Écaille

Anse de Petit Cul-de-Sac

Grand-Cul-de-Sac

Grand Fond

Petit-Cul-de-Sac

Les Petites Anses

Anse de Toiny

Anse de Grand Fond

Île Coco

Anse de Gros Jean

0   1   2km

© Ulysses Travel Publications

Some maps don't even mention Saint Barts, a tiny island covering barely 25 km^2, located at the northern end of the Lesser Antilles. Yet this island, with its fine sand beaches washed by crystalline waters, its pretty villages of orange-roofed houses and its beautiful main town, Gustavia, has a unique face that is not soon forgotten. Its inhabitants, proud descendants of the French colonists who settled here in the last centuries despite the poor soil conditions, have made this rolling land into a place like no other for connoisseurs of stunning natural landscapes. Perhaps cartographers have deliberately overlooked the island in an attempt to keep the secrets of this Caribbean paradise for themselves...

Geography

Saint Barts appeared several million years ago, when an eruption of magma forced the Atlantic plate towards the coast of the Americas where it became wedged under the smaller Caribbean plate. The

Lesser Antilles chain of islands, Saint Barts included, thus emerged from the sea.

This minuscule island, only 10 km long from one end to the other (for a total of 25 km²), rises from the waves like a small mass of mountains about 30 km from Saint Martin. These mountains form the heart of this land, whose narrow, winding roads lead to collections of charming little houses. Stunted vegetation grows from the poor volcanic soil, and on the steeper slopes there is nothing but cacti and scrub. Very little of this island is suitable for agriculture, which made it less attractive to early settlers. Luckily its shores are dotted with beautiful beaches of fine sand. Those on the western *Côte sous le Vent*, or leeward side (so named because it is protected from the violent winds of the Atlantic Ocean), are washed by the calm, warm waters of the Caribbean Sea and are perfect for swimming. The beaches on the eastern *Côte au Vent*, or windward side, meet the Atlantic Ocean head on, and are whipped by rough waves caused by the ocean winds. Together these beaches make Saint Barts a veritable vacationer's paradise.

■ Flora

Stunted plant-life is all that can be sustained by the minimal rainfall found on Saint Barts. Small shrubs and cacti do their best to adapt to the volcanic soil. In certain places, plants appear to be growing right out of the rock. Among the species that have adapted to this arid land are the latania (the woven straw of which is used to make pretty crafts) and the white frangipani.

A different type of vegetation, made up of creepers and seagrape trees, flourishes along the edge of the beaches. The seagrape is easily recognizable by the clusters of large green fruit, similar to grapes, to which it owes its name. Another tree occasionally found near beaches is the dangerous manchineel, which produces a caustic sap that can cause serious burns. It is usually marked by a red X or a sign, but can also be identified by its small round green leaves bisected by a yellow vein.

An incredible profusion of multi-coloured flowers covers the country-side. The hibiscus is the most widespread flowering tree on the island, lending its red glow to gardens year-round. Imported from tropical Asia, these bushes were planted in the 18th century. Saint Barts' gardens are also adorned with the vibrant hues of flamboyants and bougainvillea.

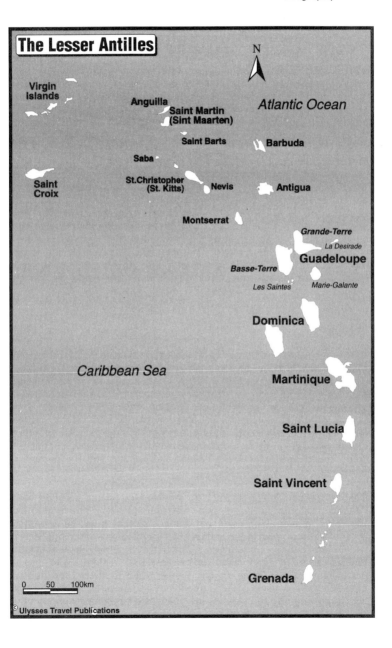

■ The Mangrove Swamp

There are mangrove swamps near Grand Cul-de-Sac, Grande Saline and Saint-Jean. This strange forest grows in the mud and salt water and consists of only a few varieties of mangrove, recognizable by their large aerated roots which plunge into the submerged earth. Shrubs and plants are often found in these swamps as well, creating an impenetrable tangled mass of roots and vegetation. Various species of birds, crustaceans and above all insects live in the heart of this swamp.

■ The Ocean Floor

The shallow, perpetually warm waters around Saint Barts provide a perfect environment for the growth of coral, formed by a colony of coelenterate polyps growing on a polypary (calcareous skeleton). Sea anemones and gorgonian coral can be viewed up close amidst the coral, which is still abundant on the continental shelf, but unfortunately in worse shape near shore. The abundant plankton around these formations attracts a wide variety of marine wildlife. Skin-diving is a great way to explore this fascinating underwater world of strange shapes and spectacular colours.

■ Fauna

Like other islands of the Lesser Antilles, this volcanic island forced from the sea, is home to a very limited number of mammals. In fact, besides domestic animals, there are only small rodents (rats and mice). Reptiles are more common. Notable specimens include the impressive iguana, which can grow to up to 1 m long. Unfortunately, this harmless animal, which feeds only on plants and insects, is an endangered species, due to over-hunting. A large number of other lizards also frequent this sun-drenched land, including ground-chameleons, found mostly near the beach, chameleons and the nocturnal moubaya.

Despite the paucity of landlubbing wildlife, the island abounds with winged creatures. There are many different species, some found near the fields, others along the coast. Patient watchers will be rewarded by the sight of tiny green iridescent hummingbirds feeding on the nectar of flowers; turtledoves, identifiable by their black-speckled maroon plumage; the small yellow-breasted sunbird, who has a particular fondness for cane sugar; slender white-feathered and orange-beaked egrets wading about; streamlined frigate birds, which can be spotted diving into the waves, and finally the famous pelican, symbol of the island, also found at the water's edge.

Pelican

History

■ Discovery of the Antilles

The morning of August 3rd, 1492, Christopher Columbus set sail on his first voyage west in search of a new route to Asia. This first crossing of the Atlantic Ocean lead him to the Caribbean archipelago, and more specifically to the island of Hispaniola (Dominican Republic and Haiti). Having discovered these islands, which he believed to be rich in gold, Columbus excitedly returned to Spain. The success of this first trip allowed him to embark shortly thereafter on a second voyage to the Americas.

This second expedition started with a stop in Hispaniola. Though the natives of this island, the Arawaks, told him of fierce, "flesh-eating" tribes on the other islands to the south, Columbus decided to continue exploring in that direction, thus discovering the chain of islands now known as the Lesser Antilles. He reached Dominica first, then Marie-Galante (named after the ship the *Maria Galante*). Finding no potable water on either, he continued to the neighbouring island, Guadeloupe, where he stopped to replenish his stock of fresh water before continuing his journey. In November, 1493, after sailing about for several days, he came upon a tiny island which he christened Santo Bartoloméo after his brother. No doubt because there were not enough

The Daily Life of the Caribs

The Caribs lived on fertile lands that provided food in such abundance, that men had spare time for various activities. They spent their day hunting or fishing and passed the rest of the time playing the flute, meditating or making kitchen utensils; some even trained parrots. When they felt the urge, they did not hesitate to set off to war against tribes from the neighbouring islands, who lived in fear of them. Most of the daily chores, from hard labour in the fields to maintaining the household and educating the children, were entirely left to the women, who also developed a method of weaving hammocks (these cotton hammocks were quickly adopted by European sailors to make life at sea more comfortable). The workforce was large, since many of these women had been abducted from Arawak tribes. Thus was the division of labour between the sexes in Pre-Columbian times.

men to populate these islands, neither Guadeloupe nor Saint Barts were colonized at this time. With its mere 25 km², Saint Barts would long remain nothing more than a stopping point for navigators plying the waters of the region.

■ The Caribs: An Island People

When Columbus and his men visited the Lesser Antilles, the archipelago was inhabited by Amerindian tribes, the Caribs. These populations seem to have come from South America and were descendants of the Galibis, who inhabited the region between the Orinoco and Amazon rivers. They apparently displaced the Arawak tribes that already lived on the islands. The Caribs are known to have been warlike and in fact came to control all of the Lesser Antilles, including "Ouanalao", the Carib name for Saint Barts.

Not wanting to fall under the yoke of the invaders, as the Arawaks of the Greater Antilles had after the arrival of the Spanish (the Amerindians of Hispaniola were harshly treated), the Caribs banded together to halt all attempts at colonization and attacked Europeans looking to settle in the region. This perseverance proved successful, for the Caribs were hardly disturbed by the European conquerors during the early years of colonization, aside from a few quick raids on the islands (Marie-Galante and Guadeloupe).

■ The Colonization of Saint Barts

Only the Spanish and Portuguese succeeded in colonizing the New World in the 15th century. Their boats arrived in Europe full of treasures taken from the Amerindian tribes, and quickly became the target of smugglers and pirates who crisscrossed the seas making off with the spoils. It was these treasures plundered from the Spanish that showed the rest of Europe the riches to be reaped by claiming these lands to the west.

As of the 17th century, Spain's and Portugal's economies began to deteriorate, while those of France, England and Holland grew rapidly, with their merchant class getting richer and richer. The creation of trading companies with real governmental powers, such as the administration and development of various territories, favoured the growth of colonies. In France, the founding of the *Compagnie de Saint-Christophe* set in motion the French colonization of the Antilles. The first expedition did not unfold as expected, however: the company's boat was attacked by the Spanish shortly after leaving France and suffered considerable damage forcing it to stop at the first island it encountered. This island was christened Saint-Christophe (Saint Kitts, south of Saint Barts). French and English colonists already lived there, but this posed no problem for the head of the company, D'Esnambuc, who made a deal with the English to divide the island. Despite the sporadic replenishing of supplies and difficult living conditions, his men remained on the island. The original company was replaced by the *Compagnie des Îles d'Amérique* in 1635, which in turn promoted the growth of the French colonies.

This first attempt encouraged the government and French companies to continue exploring the Lesser Antilles. Soon, two men, Sieur Liénart de l'Olive and Sieur du Plessis, convinced the *Compagnie des Îles d'Amérique* of the necessity of colonizing Guadeloupe. Accompanied by 500 men and a few representatives of the church (including Père Duterte), they arrived on the 28th of June, 1635. Unfortunately, the men found it difficult to adapt to the new environment, and had to cope with inadequate provisions, epidemics and famine. Furthermore, establishing this new colony involved waging a difficult war against the Caribs, thus creating an unstable situation for the settlers. With the death of these two men, the company had to choose someone to govern the island. This was a difficult task, since the person in question would have to put the company's interests before his own.

In 1638, while the seat of the colonies still remained in Saint-Christophe, Poincy de Lonvilliers was named governor. He came up with a plan to transfer the capital to Guadeloupe, thus favouring the development of the latter from then on. The plan, however, was not brought to fruition, for it was hindered by conflicts between the governor's personal interests, those of the company executives in France and those of the company representatives in the islands. These conflicts ushered in a period of instability for the colonists of Saint-Christophe. Nevertheless, Poincy sent Sieur Jacques de Gente and about fifty colonists to populate Saint Barts. They landed on the island in 1648.

Agreements aimed at ending the war between the French and the Caribs were reached in 1641, and the colony experienced a period of peace. The respite was welcomed both by the colonists, who needed time to get settled, and the *Compagnie des Îles d'Amérique*, which found the colonies expensive. Famine, war against the Caribs, bad weather and countless other problems eventually forced the company to sell its possessions. It sold Saint-Christophe in 1647, and then gave up its other islands. Saint Barts became a possession of the Order of Malta in 1651.

This period of peace was not without its problems, as tensions between the French and Caribs continued. In 1656, the Caribs, wishing to avenge the destruction of their village by the colonists, sought retribution against the French colony. They overtook the shores of Saint Barts and massacred all of its inhabitants.

The island was soon repopulated, however; in 1659 a second group of Bretons, Normans and Poitous settled here. They founded another small French colony, which managed to survive the test of time.

The Order of Malta

The Order of Malta was founded during the Crusades to protect and care for pilgrims on their way to Palestine (1113); it was originally called the "Knights of the Hospital of Saint - John of Jerusalem". Despite their active role, the knights had to withdraw when the Holy Land was lost. The Order thus relocated to Cyprus. It wasn't until 1530, when Charles the Fifth gave up the island of Malta, that these knights took the name "the knights of Malta". At the time Saint Barts was purchased, the Order was rich and powerful.

The Caribbean colonies continued to develop despite all of this, but their economic situation remained precarious. Colbert, who began looking after France's interests in 1661, decided to create a powerful company backed by the king, which would unite all of the French colonies. The *Compagnie des Indes Occidentales* was established on the 13th of May, 1664. On the 10th of July that same year, Guadeloupe, Martinique and Saint-Christophe were bought by the company; the following year it purchased Saint Barts and Saint Martin. Although the company had a monopoly on trade between these islands and France's colonies in the Americas, it enjoyed only middling success and eventually had to cease operations. In 1674, the company's possessions were transferred to the French crown.

The colonization of the Antilles also had heavy consequences for the Carib tribes, which were mercilessly attacked by colonists looking to appropriate their lands. Outnumbered by French troops, these tribes were soon decimated. In 1660, the Caribs were deported from all French possessions and relocated to Dominica and Saint Vincent. Their descendants can still be found in Dominica today.

■ Saint Barts: A French Land

While the governors tried to get richer, newly arrived colonists in the Antilles had to settle in and develop crops that would make them self-sufficient, since it was always difficult to secure supplies from France. Crops like yams, peas and cotton permitted the inhabitants of Saint Barts to sustain themselves and also make some money, though not much, by selling their products to France.

The introduction of sugar cane to the Antilles in 1644 shook up the economy of the islands, as sugar was becoming more and more prized on the European market, making for handsome returns for the colonists. The harvesting of this plant required a large workforce, however. Since there were too few inhabitants on the islands at the time, efforts were made to increase populations. A solution was found: massive numbers of black slaves were brought over. From then on, things worked very differently in the islands. Saint Barts was an exception, its soil received too little rain to sustain the growth of sugar cane. For this reason the population of Saint Barts, like that of Les Saintes, continued to consist mainly of colonists from Normandy, Brittany and Poitou, and therefore grew very slowly.

Even though sugar cane and cotton sold well, the islands continued to have economic difficulties, linked essentially to French policies. The basis of these problems was the *"pacte coloniale"* (instituted by France), which decreed that no Caribbean products could be exported to France. Of course, this restriction seriously hindered the development of colonial markets. The justification for the policy was that the colonies must in no way interfere with the French economy. The ensuing colonists' protests were not in vain, however, and a few concessions were made, first in 1663, when exchanges were permitted between New France and New England, and then in 1784.

■ Nearly a Century of Swedish Colonization

During the 18th century, the colony prospered little and, despite a few English incursions, remained French. At the end of the Seven Years War (Treaty of Paris, 1763), France lost out to the British conqueror. Although it retained its Caribbean colonies, it had to give up its North American possessions. The residents of Saint Barts remained subjects of the King of France, but only for a few years, since in 1785 Louis XVI exchanged the island for the right to trade with Sweden and thereby acquired a warehouse of Gothenburg.

This exchange was beneficial to Saint Barts, at least as far as its economy was concerned. As of 1785, the island became a free port, which allowed Gustavia to receive many boats and take advantage of a large and lucrative black market. The island enjoyed unprecedented prosperity right up until the day after the French Revolution. Its port was then abandoned in favour of other islands.

In addition to its declining economy, Saint Barts was hit by unsettling natural disasters, making it a less promising possession. For this reason, Sweden ceded Saint Barts back to France on August 10, 1877 in exchange for 400,000 F. The treaty was ratified by a majority of the population, who became French once again. As a result, the island was administratively tied to Guadeloupe.

Over the centuries, Saint Barts had avoided the crises that rocked Guadeloupe. These years, however, were critical to the evolution of Guadeloupe, which was torn apart by racial tension between white landowners and black slaves, and by the necessity to reform an economy based on a servile workforce. A decree in 1848 officially abolished slavery in the Caribbean colonies and put an end to the existing system. Guadeloupe was thus forced to adapt to this new reality, and its already weak economy fell apart. In 1877, therefore, Saint Barts found itself bound to a colony that had just undergone some very troublesome years.

Important Dates in the History of Saint Barts

1493: Christopher Columbus discovers the Lesser Antilles, including Guadeloupe, Marie-Galante, La Désirade, Les Saintes, Saint Barts and Saint Martin. At the time, the islands are inhabited by Carib Amerindians.

1635: The Compagnie de Saint-Christophe *gets French colonization underway in the Caribbean.*

1648: A first group of colonists settles on Saint Barts, but is massacred by the Caribs.

1651: Saint Barts becomes a possession of the Order of Malta.

1660: The Carib tribes are decimated or deported from the French territories to Dominica.

1664: Colbert sets up the Compagnie des Indes Occidentales, *which attempts to promote the development of the colony.*

1674: Following the bankruptcy of the Compagnie des Indes Occidentales, *the Caribbean possessions become attached to the French Crown.*

1785: Saint Barts is sold to the Swedish for the French right to trade in Swedish territory.

1848: Slavery is definitively abolished in Guadeloupe and Martinique.

1877: Sweden cedes Saint Barts back to France.

1946: Guadeloupe and Martinique become overseas French departments. Saint Barts is administratively tied to Gaudeloupe.

■ The 20th Century and Its Crises

Major crises struck the Caribbean sugar cane industry in the late 19th and early 20th centuries. Beet sugar and overproduction in other countries forced down the price of local sugar, thus causing a major upset in the islands' economies. The industry was greatly disrupted, and the collapse of several factories led to great social hardship. Saint Barts did not have a sugar cane industry and therefore did not experience the crisis that rocked its neighbouring islands. Its economy survived due to the meagre revenue brought in by farming and fishing.

When the Great War broke out in 1914, Guadeloupe and its dependencies sent their own contingents of soldiers to support France's efforts (25 men came from Saint Barts). Casualties were high in this war and losses were considerable in these small Caribbean communities (six men did not return to Saint Barts).

The period between the two World Wars was beneficial for the economy of the island, thanks to American Prohibition. Sailors profited from the lucrative traffic of illegal alcohol with the United States. Before long, another catastrophe rocked Europe: the Second World War, which began on September 3rd, 1939. Less than a year later, on June 6th 1940, France fell to the Germans. The French colonies were thus administered by the Vichy government. France was liberated on May 8th, 1945.

On March 19th, 1946, an important law concerning Guadeloupe, its dependencies and Martinique was adopted, when these colonies were established as overseas French departments or *départements français d'outre-mer*. Saint Barts became a canton of Guadeloupe. During the following decades, especially after the 60s, all sorts of political groups demanded autonomy for Guadeloupe, a cause that left most inhabitants of Saint Barts indifferent. Since farming was still unprofitable for the island, many residents slowly began turning towards an activity that would prove much more lucrative: tourism.

Economy

As a colony, Saint Barts, with its poor soil and frequent droughts, was not affected by the ups and downs of the sugar and rum industries, the way Guadeloupe and Martinique were. A few crops, like cotton and then pineapple in the 19th century, made colonists self-sufficient. Besides farming, islanders profited from another natural resource that proved more beneficial, the sea, which allowed some to survive on fishing and others to make a living from the port infrastructures. The free zone status of the port attracted many vessels in transit. During the 20th century, the residents of Saint Barts have taken advantage of one of their most beautiful resources, nature, by turning to the lucrative tourist industry.

Political Institutions

Since the law of March 19th, 1946 came into effect, Guadeloupe has been a *département français d'outre-mer* or DOM, and Saint Barts a canton. In 1963, Saint Barts was elevated to a *sous-préfecture* (the *sous-préfecture* of the northern islands is made up of Saint Barts, Tintamarre and Saint-Martin). In accordance with the Constitution, it has two political assemblies: the *Conseil Régional*, based on a system of proportional representation, and the *Conseil Général*, elected by a two-round majority vote. The *Conseil Régional* handles economic and regional development and workforce training, while the *Conseil Général* looks after social concerns. These two assemblies have the power to legislate within their respective domains and determine appropriate budgets as well. Besides the *Conseil Régional* and the *Conseil Général*, the department has a *Comité Économique et Social* and a *Comité de la Culture et de l'Evironnement*. Four deputies represent the island in the French *Assemblée Nationale*, and two senators in the *Sénat*. Like citizens of the mainland, islanders benefit from social programs established by the French state, notably old-age pensions, family benefits, unemployment insurance and health insurance. However, these programs are not always applied according to the same norms and criteria followed in France.

Integration, Autonomy and Independence

The debates continue. The political status of Guadeloupe has been continuously called into question since the island was integrated into the French nation in 1946. Can these islands, attuned to the Caribbean way of life and located 7,000 km from France, be satisfied with their status as overseas departments and the limited powers that that entails? Many don't think so. As soon as the department was created, autonomist movements started to take shape, the most powerful being the *Parti Communiste Guadeloupéen*. Because autonomists feel that integration does not recognize the distinct character of Guadeloupan society, they are demanding new political ties with France within a federal structure. These autonomist demands, however are not favoured by Saint Barts, whose 95% white population is proud of its Norman, Breton and Poitevin origins. In fact, this population, which was never enslaved and thus has no bitter recollections of colonialism, is far from dreaming of a Guadeloupan nation.

Population

A strong majority of Guadeloupe's population is either black (descendants of African slaves brought over during the 17th and 18th centuries and at the beginning of the 19th) or mulatto (a mix of African and European origins), but in Saint Barts it is a whole other story: 95% of the 5,000 or so inhabitants are white. More than three quarters are Catholic, and French is the official language. The literacy rate, life expectancy and infant mortality rate are almost the same as in France.

PRACTICAL INFORMATION

T ravelling throughout Saint Barts is easy either by yourself or with an organized tour. This section will help you prepare your trip and familiarize you with some of Saint Barts' local customs.

Entrance Formalities

Before leaving, ensure that you bring all required documents to enter and leave Saint Barts. Keep these documents in a safe place during your trip.

■ Passport and Visas

Canadians, Americans, Swiss and members of the EEC are admitted without a visa for stays of up to 3 months. Other travellers are admitted for three weeks. They must have in their possession a valid passport for the length of their stay. French visitors only need their *carte nationale d'identité*. As well, all visitors (except French) must have a return or ongoing ticket.

These regulations could change at any time, and travellers are advised to check with the French embassy or consulate before leaving.

It is also a good idea to keep a photocopy of the pertinent pages of your passport, as well as your passport number and its expiry date somewhere safe, in case it is lost. If this should happen contact your country's embassy or consulate in order to have it replaced.

■ Customs

All Canadian, American, and Swiss visitors aged 17 and older are allowed onto the island with one litre of liquor, 2 litres of wine and 200 cigarettes or 100 cigarillos or 250 g of tobacco.

Citizens of legal age from countries that are members of the EEC are allowed 1.5 litres of spirits, 4 litres of wine and 300 cigarettes or 150 cigarillos or 400 g of tobacco.

Embassies and Consulates

Consulates can be an invaluable source of help to visitors who find themselves in trouble. For example, consulates can provide names of doctors or lawyers in the case of death or serious injury. However, only urgent cases are handled. It should be noted that the cost of these services is not absorbed by the consulates. There are no consular offices in Saint Barts, the closest one is therefore given.

■ Foreign Embassies

Australia
Bridgetown, suite 209
106 Saddle Road
Maraval, Box 3372
Trinidad and Tobago
☎ (809) 622-7320
⇄ (809) 622-8692

Belgium
1 Passe Dessart
ZI Jarry
97152 Pointe-à-Pitre
☎ (590) 26.60.18
⇄ (590) 26.87.20

Canada
72 South Quay
Box 1246
Port-of-Spain, Trinidad and Tobago
☎ (809) 623-7254 and 625-6734
⇄ (809) 624-4016

Germany
Box 828
Port-of-Spain, Trinidad and Tobago
☎ (809) 628-1630
⇄ (809) 628-5278

Great Britain
British High Commission
Lower Collymore Rock
Box 676
Bridgetown City, Barbados
☎ (809) 436-6694

Netherlands
4446, Avenue Maurice Bishop
Fort-de-France, Martinique
☎ (596) 63.30.04
⇄ (596) 63.42.65

Switzerland
21, de la Jambette
Le Lamentin, Martinique
97232
☎ (596) 50.12.43

United States
14, rue Blénac BP 561
Fort-de-France, Martinique
97206
☎ (596) 63.13.03
⇄ (596) 60.20.80

■ **French Tourist Information Abroad**

Australia
Maison de la France
BNP Building - 12th floor
12 Castlereagh Street
Sydney NSW 2000
☎ (61) 2.231.52.44
⇄ (61) 2.221.86.82

Belgium
Maison de la France
21, avenue de la Toison-d'Or
1060 Brussels
☎ (32) 513.73.89
⇄ (32) 514.33.75

Canada
Maison de la France
1981, avenue McGill College
Montréal, Québec
H3A 2W9
☎ (514) 288-4264
⇄ (514) 845-4868

Maison de la France
30 St. Patrick Street Suite 700
Toronto, Ontario
M5T 3A3
☎ (416) 593-4723
⇄ (416) 979-7587

Germany
Maison de la France
Westendstrasse 47 -
Postfach 100128
D 6000 Frankfurt AM Main 1
☎ (49) 69.75.60.83.30
⇄ (49) 69.75.21.87

Great Britain
Maison de la France
178 Picadilly
London WIV OAL
☎ (44) 71.493.66.94
⇄ (44) 71.493.65.94

Netherlands
Maison de la France
Prinsengracht 670 -
1017 KX Amsterdam
☎ (31) 20.620.31.41

Switzerland
Maison de la France
2, rue Thalberg
1201 Geneva
☎ (41) 227.328.610 and 227.
313.480

Maison de la France
Bahnofstrasse 16
Postfach 4979
CH 8022 Zurich
☎ (41) 211.30.85
⇄ (41) 212.16.44

United States
Maison de la France
610 Fifth Av. Suite 222
New York, New York
10020-2452
☎ (212) 757-1125
⇄ (212) 247-6468

Maison de la France
645 North Michigan Avenue
Chicago, Illinois
60611-2836
☎ (312) 337-6301
⇄ (312) 337-6339

Maison de la France
9454 Wilshire Bld
Beverly Hills, California
90212-2967
☎ (310) 271-7838
⇄ (310) 276-2835

Maison de la France
2305 Cedar Springs Road
Suite 205, Dallas, Texas
☎ (214) 720-4010
⇄ (214) 720-0250

■ **Tourist Information Office on Saint Barts**

Quai du Général De Gaulle
Gustavia
97095
☎ 27.87.27
⇄ 27.74.47

Entering the Country

The international airport on the island can only handle small planes. Many tourists, therefore, arrive on the island by boat, either on the ferry from Saint Martin or on a cruise ship.

■ By Plane

The airport on Saint Barts cannot handle big planes, so most visitors from North American or Europe must stop over on Saint Martin or Guadeloupe, and arrive on Saint Barts by twin engine plane. Even though it is tiny, the airport offers all the services a traveller might need in the way of shops, airline company and car rental offices.

Travellers can get information by phone:

General Information
☎ 27.65.41

Airline Companies

Air Guadeloupe	Air Saint-Barth	Winair
☎ 27.61.90	☎ 27.71.90	☎ 27.61.01

Car Rental Companies

All the representatives have their offices in a building adjacent to the airport. They are all set up right next to each other and all offer similar prices. There is little variance in the model of car offered, basically you have the choice between a *MOKE*, a small all-terrain vehicle with a soft top, or a *Suzuki Sidekick*.

Avis	Hertz
☎ 27.71.43	☎ 27.71.14
Budget	Island Car Rental
☎ 27.66.30	☎ 27.70.01
Europcar	Soleil Caraïbe
☎ 27.73.33	☎ 27.67.18

How to exit the airport

The airport is about 2 km from Saint-Jean and Gustavia. If you have rented a car or scooter, as you exit the parking lot, turn left to reach Saint-Jean, and right to reach Gustavia.

You can also take a taxi, since there is a depot at the airport. Call ☎ 27.75.81 to reserve one.

■ By Boat

Several cruise lines criss-cross the Caribbean making stop-overs in Saint Barts. Ships like the *Sea Goddess*, the *Renaissance*, the *Star Flyer* and the *Sun Viking* can take you to the island via the port of Gustavia. From there you can shop or enjoy one of the beautiful beaches of the area.

Between Saint Martin and Saint Barts

Several people arrive on the island via the ferry from Saint Martin. The ferry can also be used for a visit to the island of Saint Martin. Reserve a whole day for such an excursion, since the islands are about 30 km apart.

*Boats leave every day from Gustavia and reach the island in about 90 minutes. The seas are often quite high (especially in the summer) and the trip can be rough for those with queazy stomachs... (bring along some motion sickness pills). Seafaring types will find the crossing spectacular and worth every minute. All companies offer the trip for 270 F return. Among these companies, **Saint-Barth Express** (☎ 27.77.24) and **Dauphin II** (☎ 27.77.24) are worth mentioning.*

Insurance

■ Cancellation Insurance

Cancellation insurance is usually offered by the travel agent when buying your airline ticket or your trip. It allows you to be reimbursed for the ticket or trip if your vacation must be cancelled due to serious illness or death. Healthy people will probably have little need to resort to this protection, but it is always very useful to have.

■ Theft Insurance

Most house insurance policies in North America protect some of your goods from theft, even if the theft occurs outside the country. To make a claim, you must fill out a police report. It may not be necessary to take out further insurance, depending on the amount covered by your current house insurance policy. European visitors should ensure that their insurance policy protects their goods when they are abroad.

■ Life Insurance

Several airline companies offer a life insurance plan included in the price of the airplane ticket. However, many travellers already have this type of insurance and it is therefore not necessary for them to purchase more insurance.

■ Health Insurance

Before leaving, it is strongly recommended that you verify that you are adequately insured in case you should become ill. It is easy to purchase health insurance before leaving. Your insurance plan should be as complete as possible because health care costs increase rapidly in Saint Barts. When buying insurance, make sure it covers all types of medical costs, such as hospitalization, nurse's services and doctor's fees. Make sure your limit is high enough, as these fees are expensive. A repatriation clause is also a good idea in case the required care is not available on site. Furthermore, you may have to pay these costs before leaving the clinic; verify what your policy provides for in this case. During your vacation, keep proof of your insurance policy on you, so that if you need it, you can avoid any problems.

Health

It is not necessary to protect yourself against any infectious diseases before travelling to Saint Barts. People arriving from areas infected with yellow fever must be vaccinated against it.

Some sanitary precautions should be taken to avoid certain illnesses. Below is a brief description of some of these precautions.

Consumption of too much alcohol can cause illness, especially when coupled with overexposure to the sun.

Most problems are related to digestion. Different food and exposure to sun can have averse effects on some people.

■ Health Care

Quality health care is available throughout the island. Do not hesitate to go to the nearest clinic if you need to consult a doctor. There is no need to worry when it comes to drugstores either; they are numerous and sell all the latest medicines.

Gustavia

Hôpital de Bruyn
Rue Sadi Carnot
☎ 27.93.11

Pharmacie St Barth
Rue de la République
☎ 27.61.82

Saint-Jean

Pharmacie de l'aéroport
☎ 27.66.61

■ Insects

Insects are abundant everywhere on the island and can be quite unpleasant. They are particularly numerous during the rainy season. To minimize the chances of being bitten, cover yourself well, avoid bright-coloured clothing, do not wear perfume, and use a good insect repellent. Remember, insects are more active at sundown. When walking in the mountains and forest areas, wear shoes and socks that protect your feet and legs. It is also advisable to carry ointments that will soothe the irritation caused by bites. Coil repellents will allow you to enjoy evenings on a terrace and in your room with the windows open.

■ The Manchineel

This tree of the euphorbiacous family produces a poisonous sap that causes serious burns. It has been systematically removed from the beach areas but a few remain in certain places. Most of these have been marked by a red stripe of paint or a sign. They are recognizable by their small round leaves with a yellow central vein. Both the tree trunk and the leaves are dangerous, so do not touch them. Avoid using them for shelter during rain showers because the drops of rainwater carry the poisonous sap and can burn you. Furthermore, eating the fruit of this tree is also dangerous. If you do sustain a burn from this tree, or eat the fruit, consult a doctor immediately.

■ The Sun

Despite its benefits, the sun causes several problems. Always bring a sun screen that protects against the sun's harmful rays and apply it 20 to 30 minutes before exposure. Too much exposure can cause sunstroke (fainting, vomiting, fever, etc.), especially the first few days. It is important to protect yourself to avoid the problem, and to allow time to get used to the sun. Sunglasses and a hat can help protect against the harmful effects of the sun.

■ The First Aid Kit

A small first aid kit can help you avoid many difficulties; prepare it carefully before leaving on your trip. Ensure that you have enough of all your regular medications, as well as a valid prescription in case you lose this supply. Other medication, such as Imodium or an equivalent, should also be bought before leaving. In addition, bring adhesive bandages, disinfectants, analgesics, antihistamines, an extra pair of glasses and pills for upset stomach.

Climate

The average temperature in Saint Barts is 26°C. The heat is never stifling, as regular breezes and trade winds, come from the east and north-east. There are however, still two seasons in Saint Barts. The dry season is the more pleasant of the two because the heat is less intense, there is less rain, and the humidity is lower. The average daytime temperature during this season is 24°C, and 19°C at night. Travelling during the rainy season is also possible because even though rain showers are heavy, they do not last long. There is more rain from August to October. This time of year is also hurricane season. During the rainy season, expect the temperature to hover at 27°C during the day and 22°C at night. The average hours of sunshine generally remain constant throughout the year.

Packing your Bags

The type of clothing required does not vary much from season to season. In general, loose-fitting, comfortable cotton clothes are the most useful. Closed shoes that cover the entire foot are preferred for walking in the city because they protect against cuts that might become infected. Bring a sweater or long-sleeved shirt for cool evenings, and rubber sandals to wear at the beach and in the shower. An umbrella is useful during the rainy season. Bring more dressy clothes if you anticipate evenings out.

Safety and Security

Like everywhere, there is a risk of theft in Saint Barts, but a bit of caution can eliminate problems. It is in your best interest to keep your electronic equipment in a nondescript bag over your shoulder, to avoid taking out all your money when buying something and to leave nothing of value visible in your car.

A money belt can be used to conceal cash, traveller's cheques and your passport. That way if your bags should happen to be stolen, you will at least have money and the necessary documents to help you out. Remember that the less attention you draw to yourself, the less chance you have of being robbed.

If you bring valuables to the beach, it is strongly recommended that you keep a constant eye on them. It is safer to keep your valuables in the small safes available at most hotels.

Transportation

There is no public transportation on the island. If you aren't renting a car or scooter, or taking a taxi, you'll have to walk or hitchhike.

■ Car Rental

There are car rental agencies in all the cities and near the tourist villages. No matter where you rent, you can expect to pay about 300 F per day (in high season) for an all-terrain vehicle (unlimited mileage), not including insurance. Occasionally it is advantageous to pay in American dollars, while some local car rental companies offer reductions on weekly rentals. Most rental offices are at the airport (see p 27).

When renting, it is recommended that you take out automobile insurance to cover all costs in case of an accident. Before signing the contract, make sure that payment details are clearly defined. Your credit card must be able to cover the rental costs as well as the insurance deductible when you sign the contract. Also, remember that gold credit cards often cover some insurance costs for car rentals. Check with your credit card company.

A valid drivers' license from your home country is acceptable.

You must be 21 years of age to rent a car.

If you are travelling during the busy season, make sure to reserve your vehicle in advance.

■ Roads

The island's road network is easy to sum up: basically one road follows the periphery of the island, and another one links Marigot and Philipsburg. There are also a few smaller roads, sometimes unpaved that lead to some of the beaches. Relatively few cars travel these narrow and often steep roads.

Additional Information for Drivers

Road signs are generally well marked and dependable; it is easy to find your way to the downtown areas of the small cities.

For the most part, roads are not well lit and they often wind through the hills, so take care when driving at night.

Do not forget that you must give right of way to traffic coming from the right. This means that at intersections, you must yield to the car on the right no matter who got there first.

When the road goes through a city or village, there will often be speed bumps. These are meant to slow traffic down to protect pedestrians. They are usually well marked, and for the most part are painted yellow. Some speed bumps, however, are poorly marked. To avoid any problems, slow down when travelling through towns especially near the touristy areas like Saint-Jean and Lorient.

To make travelling throughout the islands easier, buy the IGN (*Institut Géographique National*) map of Guadeloupe, with a 1:100,000 scale. There is also a more precise map of Saint Barts with a 1:25,000 scale.

Gas

There are two gas stations on the island; one is in Lorient, and the other is next to the airport. Both close at 5pm from Monday to Saturday and are closed on Sunday. Outside of these hours an automatic system can be used with a credit card (open all night).

■ Renting a Scooter or a Bicycle

If the open road beckons, it is easy to rent a motorcycle, a scooter or a bicycle. A scooter costs approximately 150 F per day and a bicycle costs 60 F per day. You will need to leave your drivers' license as a deposit, as well as 300 F when renting a scooter. Remember to always drive carefully, and that wearing a helmet is a good idea. Finally if you plan on renting a bicycle, take note that the terrain is quite hilly.

Gustavia

Chez Béranger
☎ 27.89.00

Fredo Moto
Rue Courbet

Saint-Jean

Ouanalao Moto
Galeries du Commerce
☎ 27.88.74

■ Taxis

Taxis are one of the most efficient ways of getting around the island since they go everywhere. Cars are easy to find near the marina in Gustavia and next to the airport in Saint-Jean.

Gustavia
☎ 27.66.31

Airport
☎ 27.75.81

■ Buses

There is no public transportation system on the island.

■ Hitchhiking

Hitchhiking is and easy way to get around. But remember that in certain areas of the island, cars pass very infrequently.

■ Table of distances

	Colombier	Grand Cul-de-Sac	Gustavia	Sait-Jean
Colombier		9 km	4 km	4 km
Grand Cul-de-Sac	9 km		8 km	5 km
Gustavia	4 km	8 km		3 km
Saint-Jean	4 km	5 km	3 km	

Money and Banking

■ Money

The French franc is the official currency on the island, but several merchants also accept the American dollar.

At press time, exchange rates were as follows:

$1 CAN	= 3.7 FF	= 1.2 fl	= $0.74 US
$1 US	= 5 FF	= 1.6 fl	
1 £	= 7.9 FF	= 2.6 fl	= $1.6 US
$1 Aust	= 3.8 FF	= 1.2 fl	= $0.76 US
100 peseta	= 4.1 FF	= 1.3 fl	= $0.81 US
1000 lira	= 3.1 FF	= 1 fl	= $0.63 US
10 BF	= 1.7 FF	= 0.6 fl	= $0.35 US
1SF	= 4.2 FF	= 1.4 fl	= $0.86 US
l fl	= 3.1 FF		= $0.63 US

Prices in the guide are in French francs.

■ Banks

There are banks near the airport and in Gustavia. All of them can change foreign currencies into francs or American dollars. Here are the addresses and opening hours of these banks:

Gustavia

Banque Française Commerciale
Rue du Général de Gaulle
7:30am to noon and 2pm to 4:30pm
☎ 27.62.62

Crédit Agricole
Rue du Bord de Mer
8am to 1pm and 2pm to 5pm, open Saturday 8am to 1pm
☎ 27.89.90

Saint-Jean

Galeries du Commerce (facing the airport)
Tuesday to Friday 8:15am to 12:15pm and 2pm to 5pm
☎ 27.65.88

■ Traveller's Cheques

It is always best to keep most of your money in traveller's cheques. Exchanging them for cash is easiest if your cheques are in French francs. Always keep a copy of the serial numbers of your cheques separate from the cheques, in case they are lost, that way the company can easily and quickly cancel the old cheques and replace them.

■ Credit Cards

Credit cards, especially Visa (Carte Bleue) and MasterCard, are accepted in most businesses. However, do not count on using them everywhere, always make sure you have some cash with you.

■ Cheques

French visitors should not count on paying with personal cheques, many businesses do not accept them because of the risk of fraud.

Mail and Telecommunications

There are three post offices on the island.

Gustavia
at the corner of Rue du Centenaire and Rue Jeanne d'Arc
8am to noon and 2pm to 4pm; closed Wednesday and Saturday pm

Saint-Jean
Galeries du Commerce
8am to noon and 2pm to 4pm; closed Wednesday and Saturday pm;
8am to 2pm in December

Lorient
7am to 11am during week, and 8am to 10am on Saturday

Phone cards for use in public phones can also be purchased at post offices. Two cards are available, one for 36 F and one for 87 F.

The area code on the island is 590.

To call abroad from Saint Barts:

- To Canada or the United States, dial 19, then 1, the area code and the phone number.
- To France (Paris-Île de France), dial 16, then 1, and the telephone number.
- To France (other regions), dial 16 and the phone number.
- To Belgium, dial 19, then 32 and the phone number.
- To Switzerland, dial 19, then 41 and the phone number.
- To Great Britain, dial 19, then 44 and the phone number.
- To the Netherlands, dial 19, then 31 and the telephone number.

To call Saint Barts from abroad:

- From Canada and the United States, dial 011, then 590 and the phone number.
- From France, dial 19 then 590 and the phone number.
- From continental Europe (Belgium, the Netherlands or Switzerland), dial 00, then 590 and the phone number.
- From Great Britain, dial 010, then 590 and the phone number.

Post offices have fax and telex machines.

A few emergency phone numbers

Ambulance or Fire
☎ 27.66.13

Police
☎ 27.66.66

Holidays

All banks and several businesses are closed on public holidays. Be sure
to change money and do your shopping the day before.

January 1	New Year's Day
Variable	Shrove Tuesday (*Mardi Gras*)
Variable	Ash Wednesday
Variable	Easter Sunday and Monday
May 1	Labour Day
May 8	Remembrance Day Armistice 1945
Variable	Ascension Day
May 27	Abolition of Slavery
Variable	Whitsun
July 14	National Holiday
July 21	Victor Schœchler Day
August 15	Assumption - Fête de Pitea
August 24	Fête de Saint-Barthélemy
November 1	All Saints' Day
November 11	Remembrance Day Armistice 1918
December 25	Christmas

Miscellaneous

■ Water

There are no rivers or streams on Saint Barts. Freshwater must be
produced by the desalination plant, it is therefore precious and not to
be abused.

■ Electricity

As in continental Europe, appliances work on 220 V (50 cycles). Even
though there are a few 110 V plugs, North Americans should bring
along a converter and an adapter.

■ **Women Travelling Alone**

Women travelling alone to Saint Barts don't need to worry: life is peaceful and violence is infrequent. Of course, the requisite amount of caution should be taken.

■ **Time Difference**

Saint Barts is on Eastern Standard time during the summer, there is no daylight savings time, so in winter the island is one hour ahead of Montréal and New York. There is six hours difference between Saint Barts and continental Europe during the summer and five hours in the winter.

■ **Weights and Measures**

Saint Barts uses the metric system.

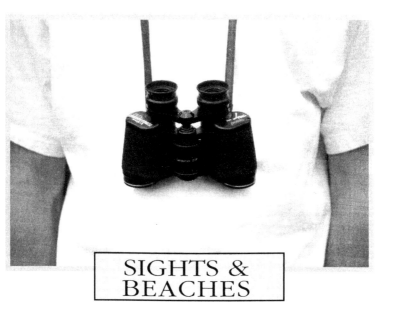

SIGHTS & BEACHES

A tour of the minuscule island of Saint Barts, with its 25 km² of hills, villages and beaches, takes little time. There are nevertheless a number of stunning locales here such as Anse de Grand Fond, Baie de Saint-Jean and of course the pretty town of Gustavia. This magnificent, sun-baked land has much to offer vacationers, and the following tour will help you discover its best sights and most beautiful beaches.

 Gustavia

The town of **Gustavia** ★★★ developed around a natural harbour, which was well-protected from sea currents and winds and thus ideal for mooring boats. This geographic feature was extremely advantageous for this tiny land, as colonists were able to establish an excellent port, where the many vessels plying the Caribbean could find safe haven. In fact the harbour was the main reason Saint Barts was colonized in the

---

Hurricane Luis

In early September 1995 (right before going to press), Hurricane Luis wreaked havoc in the Lesser Antilles, tearing through houses, pitching boats up onto dry land, uprooting trees and leaving residents without water and electricity. One of the most powerful hurricanes to pass through the Caribbean this century, Luis devastated the islands of Saint Barts and Saint Martin. However, with the passing of the storm, the reconstruction of homes and facilities was immediately undertaken.

---

first place; the island had few other resources, since its soil was very poor and received little rainfall. A town grew up around the port, and as a result of the constant activity here, bit by bit became the nerve centre of the island. However, as a strategic navigational point, the port was devastated more than once by the English (1690, 1744 and 1801).

The seaside town grew over the years, maintaining its importance when it was ceded to Sweden in 1785, but changing its name from Port Carenage to Gustavia. It prospered under the Swedes and new buildings with a distinctly different architecture were constructed. Unfortunately, few buildings remain from this period, having been destroyed by the fire that ravaged the island in 1852. The pretty green **Vieux Clocher (1)**, or old bell tower still stands on Rue du Presbytère. It once housed a bell cast in 1799, which rang off the important moments of the day. A clock has since replaced the bell. During the same period, three forts were also built on the summits of the surrounding hills to protect the Swedish colony. The fortifications of only one of these 18th century stone forts, **Fort Gustave (2)**, can be viewed today. Visitors will find a terrace offering a lovely view ★ of Gustavia. Nothing remains of **Fort Karl (3)**, while the fortifications of **Fort Oscar (4)** have been modified over the years. This last site can only be observed from afar, as it is now occupied by the Minister of Armed Forces.

When France retook possession of the island in 1878, Gustavia kept its name and its status as the principal town on the island, and the residents remained exempt from taxes. It is still the busiest and largest urban area in Saint Barts. If you arrive by boat, you will find yourself more or less at the heart of the town. It is worth exploring the few streets radiating from the harbour, all lined with pretty little white

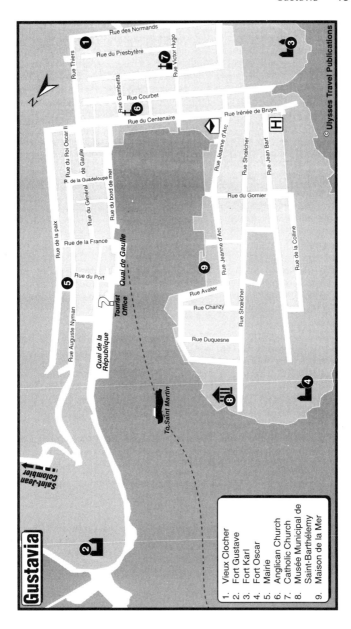

Gustavia

To Saint Martin

Saint-Jean Colombier

© Ulysses Travel Publications

Rue des Normands
Rue du Presbytère
Rue Thiers
Rue Gambetta
Rue Courbet
Rue du Centenaire
Rue Victor Hugo
Rue Irénée de Bruyn
Rue du Roi Oscar II
R. de la Guadeloupe
de Gaulle
Rue du Général
Rue du bord de Mer
Rue de la paix
Rue de la France
Rue du Port
Rue Auguste Nyman
Quai de la République
Quai de Gaulle
Tourist Office
Rue Jeanne d'Arc
Rue Shoelcher
Rue Jean Bart
Rue du Gomier
Rue de la Colline
Rue Jeanne d'Arc
Rue Avater
Rue Chanzy
Rue Shoelcher
Rue Duquesne

1. Vieux Clocher
2. Fort Gustave
3. Fort Karl
4. Fort Oscar
5. Mairie
6. Anglican Church
7. Catholic Church
8. Musée Municipal de Saint-Barthélemy
9. Maison de la Mer

houses topped by orange roofs. Wander about and explore Gustavia's
charming back streets, enjoy its cafes and good restaurants, or give in
to temptation and browse through its many shops. Besides the quaint
houses, there are some distinguished edifices, like the **Mairie (5)**, or
town hall *(Rue Auguste Nyman)*, also called the *"Maison du
Gouverneur"*, or governor's house, since the island's governors used to
reside here. The stone foundation of this house supports a lovely green
and white façade. Two other buildings are also worth a look: the
Anglican church (6) and the **Catholic church (7)**. The former stands on
Rue du Centenaire facing the sea. Built in 1885 of stone and wood, it
is topped by a pretty bell tower. It still serves a sizeable congregation.
The church is located on one of the prettiest streets in town, **Rue du
Centenaire ★**, which runs alongside the port, providing an interesting
perspective of Gustavia. The austere white façade of the Catholic
church *(Rue du Presbytère)*, the more imposing of the two, is visible in
the distance from Rue du Centenaire.

You could spend a day visiting Gustavia's sights. If you are curious
about the history, traditions and daily life of Saint Barts, head to the
Musée Municipal de Saint-Barthélemy (8) *(10 F; Mon to Thu 8am to
noon and 1:30pm to 5:30pm, Fri until 5pm, Sat 8:30am to noon; at the
end of Rue Schœlcher)*. The museum will soon move to Wallhouse, on
the waterfront, which is being renovated.

The streets bordering the natural harbour are very lively, as they are
home to pleasant shops, restaurants, the marina and, of course,
companies offering excursions at sea. Among these, the **Maison de la
Mer ★ (9)** *(6 Rue Jeanne d'Arc, ☎ 27.81.00)* provides an opportunity to
explore the sea bottom. Visitors can contemplate this fascinating world
aboard the vessel *l'Aquarius*. Comfortably seated in the hull of the boat,
passengers observe the marine life from a glass dome.

*Follow Rue Auguste Nyman out of Gustavia, past the airport and into
Saint-Jean.*

 Saint-Jean

The town of **Saint-Jean ★** lies stretched along the shore of the beautiful
Baie de Saint-Jean. Several houses, adorned with friezes and scattered
across the hillside, lend a certain style to Saint-Jean, a town that
otherwise would not amount to much more than four shopping centre:
the Galeries du Commerce, the Villa Créole, La Savane and the Centre
Commercial Saint-Jean. You will quickly discover Saint-Jean's main

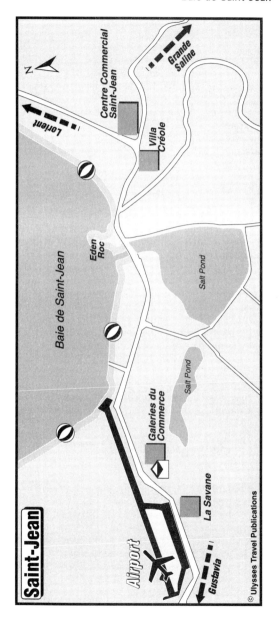

attraction hidden behind lush vegetation and a few well-located businesses: the **Baie de Saint-Jean ★★**, whose shimmering turquoise waters wash up onto a long crescent of golden sand. This virtual paradise attracts a busy crowd of sun worshippers and swimmers (park your car on the side of the road). Many are also drawn by the considerable number of comfortable hotels standing at the water's edge (see p 59). Besides the superb beach, there are the many fine restaurants along the waterfront to be enjoyed in between swims. Many claim this is the most beautiful beach on the island.

Continue toward Lorient.

 Lorient

Though the route to **Lorient** follows the sea, but all that is visible is the vegetation alongside the resort complexes and pretty residences. In certain places the road opens up onto beautiful views of the precipitous coastline plunging into the sea. On your way into the village, you'll pass a grocery store, then a little cemetery whose tombstones are adorned with plastic flowers. This cute little hamlet lies on the shores of **Anse de Lorient ★**, whose waves attract surfing enthusiasts. The beach is a popular swimming spot despite the fact that it is quite rocky. It is also highly prized by sunbathers because of its super-fine sand. There are several friendly hotels in Lorient, which is frequented by vacationers of all ages in search of a lovely beach and a peaceful spot to relax.

The road continues east to a less populated area of the island, making a loop as it passes by the beautiful beaches of Anse de Grand Cul-de-Sac, Petit Cul-de-Sac and the magnificent southeastern coast.

  Grand and Petit Cul-de-Sac

The eastern extremity of the island is punctuated by several lagoons with iridescent blue waters. Technically, these beaches are part of the windward coast, however, tucked in between the cliffs, they are protected from the strong currents and crashing waves and are therefore a haven for swimmers and amateur windsurfers. **Anse de Grand Cul-de-Sac ★★** is also the nicest beach on this part of the island. The shallow lagoon, with its limpid waters, is surrounded by hills dotted with quaint orange-roofed houses. A few hotel complexes have been built along this beautiful stretch of coastline to take advantage of this

A Tiny land with Many Faces

Despite the island's diminutive size, several linguistic distinctions exist here. Besides French, the official language, there are no less than four ways of communicating, even though villages are only a few kilometres apart. For example, Guadaloupan Creole is often heard in Gustavia, while in the windward parts of the island a Creole particular to Saint Barts is spoken. In the centre of the island, in villages like Saline and Saint-Jean, some people still speak Old French. Finally, in the western part of the island, residents use a sort of patois, a mix of the different French dialects spoken by those who settled on the island in the 18th century. These dialects, however, are gradually fading out.

divine little corner of the island. Aside from the resorts and a handful of residences here and there, the shores of this part of the island are basically undeveloped.

Just a few steps from Grand Cul-de-Sac, nestled at the base of the hills, is **Anse Marigot**. Steep cliffs rise up all around this lagoon, protecting it from the wind and making it a popular spot with both swimmers and small-boat owners, who moor their boats in its calm waters.

East of Anse de Grand Cul-de-Sac, **Anse de Petit Cul-de-Sac** is even less developed. The undergrowth and seagrape trees growing here and there provide welcome shade from the hot sun and create the feeling of a deserted beach. Anse de Petit Cul-de-Sac has all the charm of a typical Caribbean beach far from the towns and free of any touristy developments. The area has not been built up because rocks of all sizes dot the beach, making it impossible to swim here. This spot will nevertheless appeal to those in search of a secluded piece of paradise.

 Anse Toiny and Anse Grand Fond

As the road continues, the landscape changes, with beaches of fine sand gradually giving way to steep cliffs. There are no fine-sand beaches in the southeastern part of the island; **Anse Toiny** and **Anse Grand Fond** ★★ are bordered by sheer walls of rock continuously slammed by waves. The wild scene is rendered almost hypnotic by the huge, peaceful expanse of blue sea, only occasionally broken by a colourful boat going by. If you like ragged scenery, then take the time to visit this unspoilt region.

The road follows the shore from Anse Toiny all the way to Anse Grand Fond then cuts inland. It snakes through the hills, climbs abruptly at times, then zigzags downhill between beautiful residences. Touring this part of the island by bike requires a lot of stamina. The region is sprinkled with charming little houses adorned with friezes and tiny gardens where rare cultivated island plants do their best to grow and flower. As dreamily peaceful as can be, this area typifies Saint Barts perhaps more than any other.

In Petite Saline, the road splits in two, with one fork heading to Lorient and the other continuing inland; take the latter (keep left) and drive another kilometre, at most, to another fork; keep left to reach Anse de Grande Saline.

 Anse de Grande Saline

Before reaching the ocean, you'll cross the interior and come upon the huge white rectangle formed by the cloudy water of the Grande Saline. In the past, salt was extracted from this saltern, providing some residents of Saint Barts with substantial returns. The Grande Saline is surrounded by a mangrove swamp and attracts many species of birds (especially waders), which can be easily observed by anyone with a pair of binoculars. This saltern lends its name to the beach located right next to it, **Anse de Grande Saline** ★★, known for its wild beauty, the lush green hills that surround it, its fine sand and its limpid waters. Unlike such touristy beaches as Baie de Saint-Jean, an incomparable sense of nature untouched by any kind development reigns along this beautiful, tranquil stretch of sand.

To visit the western part of the island, you must return to Gustavia, or pass by the airport. Typical island houses dot the hills surrounding Gustavia. The winding road through these hills offers a bird's-eye view of the town, its orange roofs framing the harbour and the assortment of vessels moored there.

To reach Gustavia, retrace your steps and turn left at the second road. This leads into town From there follow the road to Corossol.

Mangrove

 Corossol

Corossol ★ is a tiny community that has developed on a hillside at the edge of **Anse de Corossol**. Here again, quaint little orange-roofed houses elegantly decorated with friezes brighten up an otherwise drab landscape of shrubs and undergrowth. This modest, typically Caribbean village has a certain charm, and fortunately the road running alongside the pretty beach gets little traffic. This is a wonderful place to unwind on sunny days, when colourful fishing boats bob in the water off in the distance, and the odd pelican glides by.

A small museum called the **Musée du Coquillage** ★ *(20 F; Tue to Sun 9:30am to 5pm; ☎ 27.62.97)* has opened its doors. It displays all kinds of shells (more than 400 varieties). This unique treasure was collected by the owner, M. Magras, over his lifetime.

To reach the centre of the island and the village of Colombier, return to the main road and turn left at the first intersection.

Colombier

This hamlet high in the hills in the western part of the island, has been isolated for many years even though it is only two kilometres from Gustavia. Farmers in these parts had to work hard to reap meagre livelihoods from their unproductive lands. In 1918, Père De Bruyn wanted to help these poor people, and thanks to his efforts a chapel, school and water tank were built. The chapel still stands at the centre of the village. Colombier enjoys a superb view from its perch up in the hills, where the land rolls away into the rippling waves of the big blue.

Head back down the northern coast of the island; you'll arrive at Anse des Flamands.

 Anse des Flamands

Anse des Flamands ★ is the most westerly beach on the island. It curves into a long crescent of white sand, and is dotted here and there by latania, those trees whose large palm leaves are used to make hats and baskets. The peace and quiet of this beach make it an ideal spot for swimming and enjoying a siesta in the shade of a latania tree.

 Anse des Cayes

Not far from Baie de Saint-Jean, Anse des Cayes has acquired quite a reputation for surfing and underwater fishing. Those who dream only of sunbathing will also find its fine sand to their liking.

Iguana

OUTDOOR
ACTIVITIES

With its 22 fine-sand beaches stretching along the Caribbean Sea and the Atlantic Ocean, Saint Barts is a real paradise for water-sports enthusiasts. In fact most of what there is to do in terms of outdoor activities has to do with the water. Besides enjoying the surf, you can go horseback riding and bicycling.

What follows is a listing of those activities available on the island, as well as addresses of places that rent the necessary equipment.

 ## Swimming

If swimming is your thing, then you are all set, you just have to pick the spot. Of the island's 22 beaches, 15 are great for swimming, and each is prettier than the last. The quality of the water at all of these beaches is monitored every year and found to be excellent (except at Gustavia, where it is average).

Beaches on the island are divided in two groups: those on the windward side, or *Côte au Vent*, and those on the leeward side, or *Côte sous le Vent*. Worth mentioning among the first are the beaches on Baie St-Jean, Anse Lorient, Grand and Petit Cul-de-Sac, Anse Toiny and Anse de Grande Saline; these beaches are usually pounded by rough surf, although some are protected by natural breakwaters. The second group, includes the beaches of Anse Corossol, Anse Colombier, Anse des Flamands and Anse des Cayes; unlike the others, these beaches are usually calm. Finally, take note that there are no nudist beaches on Saint Barts.

For sanitary reasons dogs are not permitted on beaches.

Descriptions of the best beaches can be found in the Sights and Beaches chapter (see p 41).

 Scuba Diving

The warm waters along the island's coasts provide an ideal environment for the development of coral, which in turn attracts all sorts of tropical fish. Droves of diving enthusiasts come here to witness this vivid underwater spectacle. There are many interesting sites to explore, such as the sea bottom and coral reefs off the beaches at Anse Chauvette, Anse Corossol, and Île de la Tortue. Excursions are also offered to the island of Tintamarre (Saint Martin) and Saba (Dutch Antilles; for experienced divers only). These expeditions include a boat trip and a picnic.

To join one of these excursions, you must be a certified diver (Padi, CMAS). If you are a beginner, you can still participate in a supervised dive, called a "baptism", to a depth of 5 m. There is little danger, as you are accompanied by a qualified guide who oversees your descent. It is best to be alone with a guide for your first dive. These diving excursions include the rental of all necessary equipment.

When diving, remember that you must not under any circumstances break the coral or touch the sea urchins (they have long spines that can cause severe injuries) or fire coral. Your guide will usually point these last species out.

The following centres organize diving excursions and "baptisms":

St-Barth Plongée
Port of Gustavia
☎ 27.31.10

Rainbow Dive
Corossol
☎ 27.91.80

Marine Service
Rue Jeanne d'Arc
☎ 27.70.34

 ## Snorkelling

It doesn't take much to snorkel: a mask, a snorkel and some flippers. Anyone can enjoy this activity, which is a great way to develop an appreciation for the richness of the underwater world. You can go snorkelling in the waters off most beaches, near the coral reefs inhabited by various underwater species. Most dive centres also organize snorkelling excursions.

Snorkelling Marina
Gustavia
☎ 27.96.68

Hookipa (equipment)
Gustavia
☎ 27.76.17

Wind Wave Power
Anse de Grand Cul-de-Sac
☎ 27.82.57

Hookipa (equipment)
Saint-Jean
☎ 27.71.31

 ## Day Cruises

Excursions aboard sailboats and yachts offer another enchanting way to freely explore the sea's sparkling waves. Some centres organize excursions.

Marine Services
Gustavia Pier
☎ 27.70.34

Kachina (catamaran trips)
Gustavia Pier
☎ 27.66.98

Saint-Barth Sports Agency
Lorient
☎ 27.68.06

Windsurfing

Several of the island's beaches are washed by calm waters, which may not satisfy seasoned sailboarders, but are great for beginners. The beaches on the windward side, especially at Anse de Grand Cul-de-Sac and to a lesser degree at Baie de Saint-Jean, are ideal for this sport.

Wind Wave Power
Grand Cul-de-Sac
☎ 27.82 57

Saint-Barth Sports Agency
Lorient
☎ 27.68.06

St-Barth Wind School
Saint-Jean
☎ 27.71.22

 Surfing

Beaches constantly whipped by strong waves are necessary for this sport. Less experienced surfers can head out to the beaches in Lorient and Baie de Saint-Jean, where the waves are less ferocious, while experts should try the rollers at the Anse Toiny beach.

Hookipa
Saint-Jean
☎ 27.67.63

Saint-Barth Sports Agency
Lorient
☎ 27.68.06

 Waterskiing

If you are in the mood to glide swiftly across the waves, then try waterskiing. Mastering this activity does require a bit of experience, but with a little patience and some good advice you should get the hang of it.

Marine Service
Gustavia Pier
☎ 27.70.34

Deep-Sea Fishing

Deep-sea fishing excursions not only offer the excitement of a big catch on the high seas, but also make for a fun outing. These trips usually last half a day. Equipment and advice are provided.

Marine Service
Gustavia Pier
☎ 27.70.36

 ## Hiking

At the centre of tiny Saint Barts, you'll find steep hills covered only with undergrowth and shrubs. Several roads run across these hills, but there are few hiking trails. Actually, there is only one in the region of Colombier. If you head off on a trek, be well-equipped (good walking shoes, light-coloured clothing and food) and well-protected from the sun (sunscreen, sunglasses and a hat) to avoid sunstroke; leave early in the morning with plenty of food and water.

 ## Bicycling

The island is criss-crossed by narrow roads that are often very steep and unshaded. It is therefore not the ideal place for bicycling. However, a bicycle can be very useful for short distances. Rentals are available in several different spots.

Ouanalao Moto
Galeries du Commerce
Saint-Jean
☎ 27.88.74

Chez Béranger
Gustavia
☎ 27.89.00

 ## Horseback Riding

A riding stable near Baie des Flamands organizes excursions on horseback. This is a pleasant way to discover another side of the island.

Ranch des Flamands
Baie des Flamands
☎ 27.80.72

ACCOMMODATIONS

S aint Barts offers an incomparable choice of fine luxury hotels, with facilities to satisfy your every need. Staying on the cheap, however, can be quite a challenge; the French bed and breakfast association, the *Gîtes de France*, has no members on the island, and there are few budget hotels.

We have listed what we believe to be the best accommodations, keeping in mind the price category, location and particular advantages of each one. Prices indicated were valid at press time, and apply to a standard room for two people during high season (January to April, 1996). They are of course subject to change at any time.

 Gustavia

The pretty down of Gustavia, with its shops, restaurants and marina, is always busy with visitors strolling about. With much to see and do,

Luxury Hotels

The hotels in this category are all outstanding in terms of comfort and quality. Their rooms are equipped with private bathrooms and air conditioning. Some offer "all inclusive" packages covering lodging and meals, while others offer rooms with kitchenettes, allowing you to save on eating out. Most of these hotels also organize all sorts of activities.

Mid-Range and Budget Hotels

Hotels in this category are found all over the island, often in beautiful locations. The rooms are comfortable and many have private bathrooms. Smaller, and with fewer services than luxury hotels, these places usually offer a good price/quality ratio.

it is a nice place to pass the day, but there isn't much reason to spend the night, when the beaches and hills surrounding the city are so much more pleasant. There are only two hotels in the centre of town. One of these, the **Presqu'île** *(330 F; ≡, tv; Place de la Parade, Gustavia 97133, ☎ 27.64.60, ⇄ 27.72.30)*, faces the marina and offers a few basic rooms. This isn't a dream hotel, but it is well worth the affordable price.

The second hotel in the centre of Gustavia is the three-story **Sunset Hotel** *(460 F; ≡, tv; Rue de la République, B.P. 102, Gustavia 97133, ☎ 27.77.21, ⇄ 27.81.59)* which also faces the marina. The rooms are well kept, and more comfortable than the Presqu'île's, ensuring a good night's sleep.

The **Carl Gustaf** *(4,000 F bkfst incl.; ≈, ≡, ℜ, ℂ; Rue des Normands, Gustavia 97133, ☎ 27.82.83, ⇄ 27.82.37)* is built on a hillside away from the downtown area, and offers an exceptional view of the town's streets and the crystalline waves of the sea. To make the most of this superb location, each villa has a lovely terrace looking out over the beautiful landscape. These units are extremely comfortable and feature a small private pool and nicely-decorated rooms with big picture windows that frame the sea.

Saint-Jean

Saint-Jean is the second largest town after Gustavia. In the centre of the village proper, which actually consists of just a few small houses, there are no hotels. All around however, beautiful fine sand beaches unfold, lined by hotels built to take full advantage of this superb location. The hotels are easy to find by following the main road, since most are clustered together; each one, however, has its own vast property to provide guests with a measure of privacy.

The **Hôtel Émeraude Plage** *(920-1,700 F; ≡, ⊗, ℜ; Baie de Saint-Jean 97133, ☎ 27.64.78, ⇄ 27.83.08)* stands in the midst of a huge garden facing Baie de Saint-Jean; it therefore boasts a delightfully peaceful setting and direct access to the beach. No fewer than 24 bungalows (some accommodating up to 4 people) are spread out on either side of the garden, all with a view of the sea. They are all functional (each has an equipped kitchen) and very comfortable, without being too luxurious.

The pretty villas of the **Filao Beach Hotel** *(1,750 F; ≡, ⊗, tv; B.P. 667, Saint-Jean 97099, ☎ 27.64.84, ⇄ 27.62.24)*, a member of the prestigious *Relais et Châteaux* association, lie nearby. They are surrounded by a pleasant garden planted with trees and bushes of all kinds, ideal for strolling about and observing the activity around the bird feeder. At the far end, you'll find a beautiful golden beach and the shimmering sea. You can drink in this beautiful sight while enjoying a meal on the hotel's terrace. This oasis of tranquility is the perfect place for a relaxing, restful vacation.

The **Tropical Hotel** *(1,030 F; ≈, ≡, ⊗, tv; B.P. 147, Saint-Jean 97095, ☎ 27.64.87, ⇄ 27.81.74)* is built on a hillside. To get there, take the road on your right on your way from Marigot (a sign indicates the way). The ideally-located buildings offer an exceptional view of the blue sea stretched out below. The charming well-maintained rooms are decorated with rattan furniture. Unfortunately, the hotel is not right on the beach, though a lovely pool makes up for this small drawback.

 Lorient

By following the main road, you'll come upon Lorient, a small hamlet with just a few houses. The beach of Anse Lorient and the charming hotels lie nearby.

The rooms of the **Hôtel La Banane** *(1,500 F pdj; ≈, ℜ, ≡; Lorient 97133, ☎ 27.68.25, ⇄ 27.68.44)* are all set up inside pretty, colonial-style Creole houses, giving the hotel even more style. The shutters, wooden walls and rustic, old-fashioned furniture fit right in, lending the place a comfortable, homey feel.

 Anse Marigot

There is a small beach along the shores of Anse Marigot, just beside it, however, is the beautiful beach of Anse de Grand Cul-de-Sac. This explains the lack of hotels along Anse Marigot. The **Sea Horse Hotel** *(1,050 F; ≡, ≈, C; Anse Marigot 97133, ☎ 27.75.36, ⇄ 27.85.33)* was built on the cliffs facing Anse Marigot, and thus enjoys an exceptionally peaceful setting. Although it is a bit far from the ocean, the buildings were designed so that each room has a balcony overlooking the glittering waves. All of the suites have kitchenettes, and for those with a craving for something grilled, barbecues are provided on a roof-top terrace.

 Anse de Grand Cul-de-Sac

The beach at Anse de Grand Cul-de-Sac is the prettiest in this part of the island, and several hotels have been built here to take advantage of this beautiful, isolated crescent of golden sand. Far from all the hustle and bustle, this beach is a real vacation paradise.

Pavilions, built in the heart of a charming garden, house the rooms of the **El Sereno** *(1,900 F; ≡, ≈, tv, ℜ; B.P. 19, Grand Cul-de-Sac 97095, ☎ 27.64.80, ⇄ 27.75.47)*. Each is nicely decorated and has a terrace adorned with rattan furniture and looking out over the shady, verdant surroundings. The pool and restaurant (La Toque Lyonnaise, see p 66) are located on a terrace look-out overhanging the waves of Grand Cul-de-Sac. This wonderfully tranquil spot affords magnificent views of the seascape.

Upon entering **Guanahani** *(2,700 F bkfst incl.; ≡, ≈, ⊗, tv; B.P. 609, Grand Cul-de-Sac 97098, ☎ 27.66.60, ⇄ 27.70.70)*, you will discover a beautiful lobby with dark floors and colourful walls, opening discreetly onto the sea. The charming villas, with their pretty white friezes and sky-blue doors, are located in a vast garden surrounding the main building. Each villa has a terrace, and the fancier ones have a private pool or a jacuzzi. The sea unfolds at the far end of the garden.

 ## Anse de Petit Cul-de-Sac

Though the beach at Petit Cul-de-Sac is wilder and less developed than the one at Grand Cul-de-Sac, its fine sand is by no means less inviting.

The **St Barths Beach Hotel** *(1,400 F; ≡, ≈, ℜ, ⊘; B.P. 580, Petit Cul-de-Sac 97098, ☎ 27.60.70, ⇄ 27.75.57)* is a white building built directly on the beach. Its geographical location is its main attraction, since the rooms are quite simple. Guests come here mainly to enjoy the sea and the friendly holiday atmosphere.

Next to the St Barths Beach Hotel, and part of the same hotel complex are the **Résidences Saint-Barth** *(1,780 F; ≡, ≈, ℜ, ⊘; B.P. 81, Petit Cul-de-Sac 97098, ☎ 27.85.93, ⇄ 27.77.59)*. Built on the hill overlooking the bay, the 21 one- two- and three-room villas all have big bay windows and a pretty terrace from which to enjoy the stunning landscape.

 ## Anse Toiny

Anse Toiny is located on the steepest shore of the island, and the rough surf makes swimming impossible. It was here, in front of the unbridled sea, that the owner of **Le Toiny** *(4,400 F; ≡, ≈, ⊗, tv, ℂ, ℜ; Anse Toiny 97133, ☎ 27.88.88, ⇄ 27.89.30)* chose to build a luxurious hotel offering unequaled comfort. Expansive suites with magnificent wood floors, elegant furniture, and wonderfully bright, airy rooms make guests feel at home. Everything is impeccable, even the bathrooms. The best thing about these villas is that the rooms all open onto a terrace; where you'll find a private pool. A cut above, Le Toiny boasts an exceptionally peaceful setting.

 ## Colombier

The adorable village of Colombier is located in the hills in the western part of the island. Erected on the outskirts of this peaceful village, the **François Plantation** *(1,500 F; ≡, ≈, tv, ℜ; Colombier 97133,*

☎ *27.78.82,* ⇄ *27.61.26)* hotel stands on a vast property planted with trees and flowering shrubs that offer welcome shade. At the heart of this verdant vegetation, you'll find a number of cosy colourful bungalows. Some look out onto the garden, while the more expensive units offer a neverending view of the sea. You'll discover an oasis of serenity here.

Anse des Cayes

The villas of the **Manapany** *(3,140 F;* ≡, ≈, ☻, ⊗, *tv,* ℜ; *B.P. 114, Anse des Cayes 97133,* ☎ *27.75.26,* ⇄ *27.75.28)* hotel lie right at the heart of the tiny and exceedingly adorable cove of Anse des Cayes. All white and overlooking the sea, they house comfortable rooms. The hotel's garden is a lovely place to stroll and forget about your worries.

Anse des Flamands

Anse des Flamands is the last long beach on the northwestern side of the island. A few hotels have taken advantage of this beautiful and secluded natural site.

The **Hôtel Baie des Flamands** *(1,200 F,* ≡, ≈, ℜ; *B.P. 68, Anse des Flamands 97133,* ☎ *27.64.85,* ⇄ *27.83.98)* consists of a small, two-story white building. The rooms are simple, but boast a view of the sea. A relaxed atmosphere prevails.

The beautiful buildings of the **St-Barth Isle de France** *(2,720 F bkfst incl.; B.P. 612, Anse des Flamands 97098,* ☎ *27.61.81,* ⇄ *27.86.83)* lie nearby. The main house was built right at the edge of the shimmering sea; to take full advantage of this stunning setting, it has a large terrace overlooking the idyllic landscape. The guest rooms are not located in this building, but in the villas scattered throughout the large property. Even though they were not built right by the sea, special touches like their beautiful furnishings, lovely draperies and large bay windows create an equally pleasant ambience.

RESTAURANTS

Saint Barts has many excellent gourmet restaurants, friendly bistros specializing in French and Creole food, and little cafes serving sandwiches and ice cream. There is fare to satisfy every taste, so you have nothing to worry about as far as your stomach is concerned.

In an effort to satisfy the needs of all readers, we have compiled a selection of restaurants for all budgets. A phone number and address is listed for each establishment. The price indicated includes a meal for two people and tip, but excludes drinks.

■ Tipping

Always check your bill to see if a service charge has already been added (usually 15% of the total). Even if one has been included, it is still customary to leave some change for the waiter after the meal; if not, a tip is expected.

■ Creole Cooking

You will no doubt have several opportunities to sample some Creole cooking during your stay. Seldom very hot in terms of spices, the traditional cuisine follows several trends, and has its roots in African, French and sometimes East Indian food. Creole *nouvelle cuisine* has been influenced by more recent cooking techniques,

Dishes are usually variations on basic fish and seafood recipes. The most commonly used fish are red snapper, shark and tuna, while crayfish and crab are the most popular seafoods. Meat and chicken are also prepared in many different ways.

■ Drinks

As local sugar cane production was abandoned in the 19th century, there is no real Saint Barts rum. That hasn't stopped this spirit from being used in a variety of drinks like a "ti-punch", "pina-colada" or a "rum punch". Imported beer, wine (from France and Chili) and liqueurs can also be purchased at restaurants and duty free shops.

 Gustavia

You won't have any trouble finding a good restaurant in Gustavia, especially at lunch time, when the terraces open up and good daily specials top the menus.

If you want to stock up on provisions, there is an A.M.C. grocery store on Rue du Général de Gaulle.

On Rue du Roi Oscar II, you'll find the **Rôtisserie-Boulangerie** *(70 F; ☎ 27.66.36)* where you can stock up on bread and deli foods for a picnic. You'll find sandwiches of all kinds, roast chicken, delicious pastries and juices; if you feel like spoiling yourself, there are also Fauchon products, imported from France, to choose from.

The nearby **Anna Banana** ice cream counter will satisfy that sweet tooth.

The **Crêperie** *(90 F; open all day; ☎ 27.84.07)*, also located on Rue du Roi Oscar II, serves scrumptious stuffed crepes. Two tables occupy an almost non-existent outdoor terrace, in any case, the simple dining room is more pleasant. This is a neat and popular place for lunch.

Coriandre *(200 F; open for lunch and supper; Rue du Roi Oscar II,* ☎ *27.93.83)* offers a deliciously different menu, featuring Thai and Vietnamese food, which is served in a simple but pretty setting.

La Crémaillère *(225 F; open for lunch and supper; Rue du Général de Gaulle,* ☎ *27.82.48)* is accessible via a narrow path that winds its way between the buildings and leads finally to a lovely interior courtyard. Cute and unassuming, this friendly restaurant has something for every taste, from mango crayfish salad to burgers and fries.

The **Repaire des Rebelles et des Émigrés** *(300 F; open all day; Rue de la République,* ☎ *27.72.48)* is another good spot in town for delicious platters of seafood and grilled fish. Enjoy these delectable dishes while taking in the sights and sounds of the marina from the terrace. This place is open first thing in the morning (breakfast is served), and doesn't close until late in the evening.

Outside of downtown Gustavia, you can try the restaurant of the **Carl Gustaf** *(700 F; open for lunch and supper; Rue des Normands,* ☎ *27.82.83)* hotel, which serves elaborate dishes prepared with finesse. The chef combines French culinary techniques and regional ingredients, particularly those from the sea. While dining, guests can enjoy an unparalleled view from the magnificent terrace overlooking the sea and marina.

 Saint-Jean

In the Villa Créole, at the centre of Saint-Jean, you'll find the **Rôtisserie-Boulangerie** *(70 F; Villa Créole,* ☎ *27.73.46)*, a specialized grocer. Like its counterpart in Gustavia, it sells sandwiches and roast chicken.

For a hearty breakfast in a friendly atmosphere, head to **La Créole** *(150 F; Villa Créole,* ☎ *27.68.09)*, which serves simple dishes like club sandwiches and *croque-monsieur*, as well as grilled fish.

Not far from the Villa Créole, **Le Pélican** *(240 F; open for lunch and supper; Saint-Jean,* ☎ *27.64.64)* is advantageously situated on the waterfront. This no doubt explains why companies offering island tours bring their customers here for lunch. The place gets quite busy, and this popularity does have its disadvantages: come at lunchtime and you'll invariably get stuck inside, since the terrace overlooking Baie de Saint-Jean is always packed. The acclaim of this eatery is also due to its menu, which includes tasty dishes like mussels, chicken with mustard sauce and crab salad.

If you are looking for quality French cuisine, you must try the restaurant at the **Filao** *(300 F; open for bkfst and lunch; Saint-Jean,* ☎ *27.64.84)* hotel at the edge of Baie de Saint-Jean. You'll be treated to fine food, all the while enjoying the beautiful panoramic view.

 Anse de Grand Cul-de-Sac

The terrace of the **Lagon Bleu** *(200 F; open for lunch; Anse de Grand Cul-de-Sac,* ☎ *27.64.80)* was built over the water, so that diners might be gently rocked by the waves. To complete this seaside ambience, the menu offers a good selection of fish dishes, including *daurade en papillote* (sea bream cooked in foil) and *salade niçoise*.

Part of the El Sereno hotel (like the Lagon Bleu), **La Toque Lyonnaise** *(600 F; open evenings; Anse de Grand Cul-de-Sac,* ☎ *27.64.80)* prepares gourmet meals worthy of the finest of palates. You'll enjoy these refined dishes seated around the pool in a distinguished festive atmosphere.

 Anse de Petit Cul-de-Sac

Le Rivage *(280 F; open for lunch and supper; Anse de Petit Cul-de-Sac,* ☎ *27.82.42)* sits at the water's edge, with its windows open to the sea so that diners can enjoy the vast expanse of shimmering blue while they savour good Creole meals. Among these local dishes are the traditional *accras*, grilled fish and *boudin créole*. Not only does the food make dining here worth your while, but the friendly atmosphere and beautiful setting add a little something extra.

 Anse Toiny

When you arrive at the gourmet restaurant **Le Gaïac** *(700 F; open for lunch and supper; Hôtel Le Toiny,* ☎ *27.88.88)*, you will be welcomed into a tastefully decorated dining room, adorned with large windows looking out onto Anse Toiny. A quick survey of the menu is enough to make you hungry. How to choose between such a vast selection of dishes, each more tempting than the last, like the large crayfish coated with gingerbread or the *poêlée de Saint-Jacques aux échalotes et aux aubergines vinaigrées* (panfried scallops with shallots and eggplant). The meal will live up to your expectations and you'll leave with fond memories of your evening at Le Gaïac.

Colombier

The restaurant in the **François Plantation** *(500 F; evenings only;*
☎ *27.78.82)* hotel has a large dining room decorated with beautiful
wooden furniture, rattan chairs and large picture windows that open
onto the garden, creating a warm ambience. In this refined setting,
patrons are treated to precisely prepared meals, worthy of the best
French kitchens.

 Anse des Cayes

The **Ouanalao** *(250 F; open for lunch and supper; Hôtel Manapany,*
☎ *27.66.55)* offers a varied menu including both Italian (all sorts of
pasta dishes), and Creole specialties. The menu thus has something for
everyone. Brunch is served on Sunday. The Manapany has another,
fancier restaurant, the **Ballahou** *(400 F; open for supper;* ☎ *27.66.55)*,
which serves fine French cuisine.

 Anse des Flamands

Case de l'Isle *(300 F; open for lunch and supper; Anse des Flamands,*
☎ *27.81.61)* is an adorable little restaurant in the Saint-Barth Isle de
France hotel. The menu consists of delicious, classic French dishes. If
you are a fan of salads or fish you are in luck, as these figure promi-
nently among the offerings.

ENTERTAINMENT

During the day, things are really hopping in Saint Barts, but as soon as the sun sets and it gets dark, the energy level comes down a notch or two. Most people head out for supper, ending the day with a good meal. There are, however, a few bars and discotheques for those who want to dance or have a drink. Aside from these few night spots, you can also celebrate during the holidays when lots of activities are organized. There is something for everyone, except perhaps gamblers looking to try their luck, as there are no casinos on the island.

 Bars and Discotheques

All of the big hotel complexes have pleasant bars, usually with a view of the sea. Two of the most enjoyable are the one at the Hôtel Filao (Saint-Jean) and the one at the El Sereno (Anse de Grand Cul-de-Sac).

There are also some bars and discotheques that are not affiliated with any hotel.

■ Gustavia

There are a few pleasant bars in town, where you can spend a pleasant evening in a relaxing setting. One of these is the terrace of the bar **Le Sélect** *(Rue France)*, which sometimes features live music on holidays.

If you prefer somewhere with a view of the marina, try **L'Escale** *(Rue Jeanne d'Arc)*. The lively atmosphere and rhythmic music set the mood. There is also a good selection of cocktails.

Le Petit Club *(☎ 26.66.33)* is a discotheque that stays open until 4am. Revellers frequent this spot in large numbers to dance the night away.

■ Saint-Jean

At **La Créole** you can either enjoy a simple meal at the restaurant or sip a cocktail in the bar. Striped parasols decorate the terrace of this friendly little spot.

Festivities

Throughout the year, various events are celebrated with parades, dancing, music and other activities. Here is a calendar of some of the happenings:

■ January

The Festival International de Musique de Saint-Barthélemy has been celebrated for two weeks in January for more than 10 years now.

■ February, March and April

Carnaval celebrations on Saint Barts last several days, starting a few days before Shrove Tuesday (*Mardi Gras*) and ending on Ash Wednesday (*Mercredi des Cendres*). The festivities include the Mardi Gras parade and the burning of Vaval, an effigy of Carnival.

■ July

Activities throughout the day on July 14th celebrate the French national holiday.

■ August

August 24th is the *Fête de Saint-Barthélemy*, one more reason to celebrate by holding regattas, games and contests. Saint Louis' Day is celebrated in Corossol, the following day, August 25th.

SHOPPING

Nothing is taxed on the island of Saint Barts, making it a veritable consumer's paradise; consequently, shopping is one of the most popular activities here, despite the high prices. To better serve visiting customers, boutiques are stocked with merchandise of all kinds: jewellery, housewares, clothing, electronic equipment, perfume and cosmetics. Most shops are located in Gustavia or in the shopping centres in Saint-Jean.

Shops open early in the morning (8am), and most close for lunch (between noon and 2pm), then reopen until 5pm or 6pm. They are closed Sundays.

Grocery Stores

Fresh bakery bread is delivered to the supermarkets every morning.

Au Fin Gourmet
Anse des Flamands
Creole and French delicacies for take-out, including delicious *boudin Créole*

Match
Large supermarket facing the airport, Saint-Jean

Stalactite
La Savane, Saint-Jean
Pastries, breads, ice cream and sorbets

Bakery
Lorient

 What to Bring Back

The boutiques are numerous, the products, countless. We have listed a few of the more interesting places, either because of the products they sell, or their prices.

■ **Clothing and Accessories**

Gustavia

Cacharel
Rue du Général de Gaulle

Gucci
Rue du Bord de Mer

Hookipa (t-shirts)
Rue du Bord de Mer

Clémentine et Julian
French children's clothing
Rue du Roi Oscar II

Pati Sérigraphie
Rue Schœlcher

Ralph Lauren
Rue Auguste Nyman

Stéphane et Bernard
Rue de la République

Saint-Jean

Black Swan
(beach wear)
Villa Créole

Le Petit Sauvage
children's clothing
near Le Village Créole

Stéphane et Bernard
La Savane (facing the airport)

Surf Shop
Villa Créole

Plein Sud
Galerie de Commerce

■ **Jewellery**

Gustavia

Bijouterie Carat
Rue de la République

Oro de Sol
Rue de la République

Cartier
Rue de la République

Shell Shop
(shell jewellery)
Rue du Général de Gaulle

Little Switzerland
Rue de France

Saint-Jean

Kornerupine
Villa Créole

■ **Perfume and Cosmetics**

Gustavia

Free Mousse
Rue Auguste Nyman

Parfums de France
Rue de Général de Gaulle

■ **Wine and Spirits**

Gustavia

Smoke and Booze
Rue du Général de Gaulle

■ **Souvenirs and Gifts**

Gustavia

La Quichenotte
Rue du Centenaire

Papagayo
Rue du Général de Gaulle

Saint-Jean

Flea Market
Villa Créole

Kino's Karavan
Centre Commercial Saint-Jean

FRENCH GLOSSARY

GREETINGS

Hi (casual)	*Salut*
How are you?	*Comment ça va?*
I'm fine	*Ça va bien*
Hello (during the day)	*Bonjour*
Good evening/night	*Bonsoir*
Goodbye, See you later	*Bonjour, Au revoir, à la prochaine*
Yes	*Oui*
No	*Non*
Maybe	*Peut-être*
Please	*S'il vous plaît*
Thank you	*Merci*
You're welcome	*De rien, Bienvenue*
Excuse me	*Excusez-moi*
I am a tourist.	*Je suis touriste*
I am American (male/female)	*Je suis Américain(e)*
I am Canadian (male/female)	*Je suis Canadien(ne)*
I am British	*Je suis Britannique*
I am German (male/female)	*Je suis Allemand(e)*
I am Italian (male/female)	*Je suis Italien(ne)*
I am Belgian	*Je suis Belge*
I am Swiss	*Je suis Suisse*
I don't speak French	*Je ne parle pas français*
Do you speak English?	*Parlez-vous anglais ?*
Slower, please.	*Plus lentement, s'il vous plaît.*
What is your name?	*Quel est votre nom?*
My name is...	*Je m'appelle...*
spouse (male/female)	*époux(se)*
brother, sister	*frère, soeur*
friend (male/female)	*ami(e)*
son, boy	*garçon*
daughter, girl	*fille*
father	*père*
mother	*mère*
single (male/female)	*celibataire*
married (male/female)	*marié(e)*
divorced (male/female)	*divorcé(e)*
widower/widow	*veuf(ve)*

DIRECTIONS

Is there a tourism office near here?	*Est-ce qu'il y a un bureau de tourisme près d'ici?*
There is no..., we have no...	*Il n'y a pas de..., nous n'avons pas de...*
Where is...?	*Où est le/la ... ?*

straight ahead	*tout droit*
to the right	*à droite*
to the left	*à gauche*
beside	*à côté de*
near	*près de*
here	*ici*
there, over there	*là, là-bas*
into, inside	*à l'intérieur*
outside	*à l'extérieur*
far from	*loin de*
between	*entre*
in front of	*devant*
behind	*derrière*

FINDING YOUR WAY AROUND

airport	*aéroport*
on time	*à l'heure*
late	*en retard*
cancelled	*annulé*
plane	*l'avion*
car	*la voiture*
train	*le train*
boat	*le bateau*
bicycle	*la bicyclette, le vélo*
bus	*l'autobus*
train station	*la gare*
bus stop	*un arrêt d'autobus*
The bus stop, please	*l'arrêt, s'il vous plaît*
street	*rue*
avenue	*avenue*
road	*route, chemin*
highway	*autoroute*
rural route	*rang*
path, trail	*sentier*
corner	*coin*
neighbourhood	*quartier*
square	*place*
tourist office	*bureau de tourisme*
bridge	*pont*
building	*immeuble*
safe	*sécuritaire*
fast	*rapide*
baggage	*bagages*
schedule	*horaire*
one way ticket	*aller simple*
return ticket	*aller retour*
arrival	*arrivée*

return	*retour*
departure	*départ*
north	*nord*
south	*sud*
east	*est*
west	*ouest*

CARS

for rent	*à louer*
a stop	*un arrêt*
highway	*autoroute*
danger, be careful	*attention*
no passing	*défense de doubler*
no parking	*stationnement interdit*
no exit	*impasse*
stop! (an order)	*arrêtez!*
parking	*stationnement*
pedestrians	*piétons*
gas	*essence*
slow down	*ralentir*
traffic light	*feu de circulation*
service station	*station-service*
speed limit	*limite de vitesse*

MONEY

bank	*banque*
credit union	*caisse populaire*
exchange	*change*
money	*argent*
I don't have any money	*je n'ai pas d'argent*
credit card	*carte de crédit*
traveller's cheques	*chèques de voyage*
The bill please	*l'addition, s'il vous plaît*
receipt	*reçu*

ACCOMMODATION

inn	*auberge*
youth hostel	*auberge de jeunesse*
bed and breakfast	*gîte*
hot water	*eau chaude*
air conditioning	*climatisation*
accommodation	*logement, hébergement*
elevator	*ascenseur*
bathroom	*toilettes, salle de bain*
bed	*lit*
breakfast	*déjeuner*
manager, owner	*gérant, propriétaire*

bedroom	chambre
pool	piscine
floor (first, second...)	étage
main floor	rez-de-chaussée
high season	haute saison
off season	basse saison
fan	ventilateur

SHOPPING

open	ouvert(e)
closed	fermé(e)
How much is this?	C'est combien?
I would like...	Je voudrais...
I need...	J'ai besoin de...
a store	un magasin
a department store	un magasin à rayons
the market	le marché
salesperson (male/female)	vendeur(se)
the customer (male/female)	le / la client(e)
to buy	acheter
to sell	vendre
t-shirt	un t-shirt
skirt	une jupe
shirt	une chemise
jeans	un jeans
pants	des pantalons
jacket	un blouson
blouse	une blouse
shoes	des souliers
sandals	des sandales
hat	un chapeau
eyeglasses	des lunettes
handbag	un sac
gifts	cadeaux
local crafts	artisanat local
sun protection products	crèmes solaires
cosmetics and perfumes	cosmétiques et parfums
camera	appareil photo
photographic film	pellicule
records, cassettes	disques, cassettes
newspapers	journaux
magazines	revues, magazines
batteries	piles
watches	montres
jewellery	bijouterie
gold	or
silver	argent

precious stones	*pierres précieuses*
fabric	*tissu*
wool	*laine*
cotton	*coton*
leather	*cuir*

MISCELLANEOUS

new	*nouveau*
old	*vieux*
expensive	*cher, dispendieux*
inexpensive	*pas cher*
pretty	*joli*
beautiful	*beau*
ugly	*laid(e)*
big, tall (person)	*grand(e)*
small, short (person)	*petit(e)*
short (length)	*court(e)*
low	*bas(se)*
wide	*large*
narrow	*étroit(e)*
dark	*foncé*
light (colour)	*clair*
fat (person)	*gros(se)*
slim, skinny (person)	*mince*
a little	*peu*
a lot	*beaucoup*
something	*quelque chose*
nothing	*rien*
good	*bon*
bad	*mauvais*
more	*plus*
less	*moins*
do not touch	*ne pas toucher*
quickly	*vite*
slowly	*lentement*
big	*grand*
small	*petit*
hot	*chaud*
cold	*froid*
I am ill	*je suis malade*
pharmacy, drugstore	*pharmacie*
I am hungry	*j'ai faim*
I am thirsty	*j'ai soif*
What is this?	*Qu'est-ce que c'est?*
Where?	*Où?*
fixed price menu	*table d'hôte*
order courses separately	*à la carte*

WEATHER

rain	*pluie*
clouds	*nuages*
sun	*soleil*
It is hot out	*Il fait chaud*
It is cold out	*Il fait froid*

TIME

When?	*Quand?*
What time is it?	*Quelle heure est-il?*
minute	*minute*
hour	*heure*
day	*jour*
week	*semaine*
month	*mois*
year	*année*
yesterday	*hier*
today	*aujourd'hui*
tommorrow	*demain*
morning	*le matin*
afternoon	*l'après-midi*
evening	*le soir*
night	*la nuit*
now	*maintenant*
never	*jamais*
Sunday	*dimanche*
Monday	*lundi*
Tuesday	*mardi*
Wednesday	*mercredi*
Thursday	*jeudi*
Friday	*vendredi*
Saturday	*samedi*
January	*janvier*
February	*février*
March	*mars*
April	*avril*
May	*mai*
June	*juin*
July	*juillet*
August	*août*
September	*septembre*
October	*octobre*
November	*novembre*
December	*décembre*

COMMUNICATION

post office	*bureau de poste*
air mail	*par avion*
stamps	*timbres*
envelope	*enveloppe*
telephone book	*bottin téléphonique*
long distance call	*appel outre-mer*
collect call	*appel collecte*
fax	*télécopieur, fax*
telegram	*télégramme*
rate	*tarif*
dial the regional code	*composer le code régional*
wait for the tone	*attendre la tonalité*

ACTIVITIES

recreational swimming	*la baignade*
beach	*plage*
scuba diving	*la plongée sous-marine*
snorkelling	*la plongée-tuba*
fishing	*la pêche*
recreational sailing	*navigation de plaisance*
windsurfing	*la planche à voile*
bicycling	*faire du vélo*
mountain bike	*vélo tout-terrain (VTT)*
horseback riding	*équitation*
hiking	*la randonnée pédestre*
to walk around	*se promener*
museum or gallery	*musée*
cultural centre	*centre culturel*
cinema	*cinéma*

TOURING

river	*fleuve, rivière*
waterfalls	*chutes*
viewpoint	*belvedère*
hill	*colline*
garden	*jardin*
wildlife reserve	*réserve faunique*
peninsula	*péninsule, presqu'île*
south/north shore	*côte sud/nord*
town or city hall	*hôtel de ville*
court house	*palais de justice*
church	*église*
house	*maison*
manor	*manoir*
bridge	*pont*
basin	*bassin*

dam	*barrage*
workshop	*atelier*
historic site	*lieu historique*
train station	*gare*
stables	*écuries*
convent	*couvent*
door, archway, gate	*porte*
customs house	*douane*
locks	*écluses*
market	*marché*
canal	*canal*
channel	*chenal*
seaway	*voie maritime*
museum	*musée*
cemetery	*cimetière*
mill	*moulin*
windmill	*moulin à vent*
general hospital	*Hôtel Dieu*
high school	*école secondaire*
lighthouse	*phare*
barn	*grange*
waterfall(s)	*chute(s)*
sandbank	*batture*
neighbourhood, region	*faubourg, quartier*

NUMBERS

1	*un*
2	*deux*
3	*trois*
4	*quatre*
5	*cinq*
6	*six*
7	*sept*
8	*huit*
9	*neuf*
10	*dix*
11	*onze*
12	*douze*
13	*treize*
14	*quatorze*
15	*quinze*
16	*seize*
17	*dix-sept*
18	*dix-huit*
19	*dix-neuf*
20	*vingt*
21	*vingt-et-un*
22	*vingt-deux*
23	*vingt-trois*
24	*vingt-quatre*
25	*vingt-cinq*
26	*vingt-six*
27	*vingt-sept*
28	*vingt-huit*
29	*vingt-neuf*
30	*trente*
31	*trente-et-un*
32	*trente-deux*
40	*quarante*
50	*cinquante*
60	*soixante*
70	*soixante-dix*
80	*quatre-vingt*
90	*quatre-vingt-dix*
100	*cent*
200	*deux cents*
500	*cinq cents*
1 000	*mille*
10 000	*dix mille*
1 000 000	*un million*

INDEX

■ GUIDES DE VOYAGE ULYSSE

□ Arizona et Grand Canyon	24,95 $
□ Balades gourmandes autour de Montréal	12,95 $
□ Côte d'Azur - Alpes-Maritimes - Var	24,95 $
□ Costa Rica	24,95 $
□ Cuba	22,95 $
□ Disney World	22,95 $
□ Équateur	24,95 $
□ Floride	29,95 $
□ Gaspésie Bas-Saint-Laurent Îles-de-la-Madeleine	22,95 $
□ Gîtes du Passant au Québec	9,95 $
□ Guadeloupe	24,95 $
□ Honduras	24,95 $
□ Jamaïque	22,95 $
□ Le Québec	24,95 $
□ Louisiane	24,95 $
□ Martinique	24,95 $
□ Mexique Côte Pacifique	24,95 $
□ Montréal en métro	14,95 $
□ Montréal	22,95 $
□ Nouvelle-Angleterre	29,95 $
□ Ontario	14,95 $
□ Ouest canadien	24,95 $
□ Panamá	24,95 $
□ Plages de la côte est de la Floride	12,95 $
□ Plages de Nouvelle-Angleterre et Boston	19,95 $
□ Portugal	24,95 $
□ Provence	24,95 $
□ Provinces maritimes	24,95 $
□ République Dominicaine	24,95 $

□ Saguenay - Lac St-Jean - Charlevoix	22,95 $
□ El Salvador	22,95 $
□ Venezuela	22,95 $
□ Ville de Québec et environs	22,95 $

■ ULYSSE PLEIN SUD

□ Carthagène	9,95 $
□ Isla Margarita	9,95 $
□ Montelimar - Nicaragua	9,95 $
□ Puerto Plata-Sosua-Cabarete	9,95 $
□ Varadero	9,95 $
□ Saint-Barthélemy	9,95 $
□ Saint-Martin	9,95 $

■ ESPACES VERTS ULYSSE

□ Motoneige au Québec	19,95 $
□ Nouvelle-Angleterre à vélo	19,95 $
□ Randonnée pédestre dans le Nord-Est des États-Unis	19,95 $
□ Randonnée pédestre au Québec	19,95 $
□ Ski de fond au Québec	19,95 $

■ JOURNAUX DE VOYAGE ULYSSE

□ Journal de voyage Ulysse	16,95 $
□ Journal de voyage Ulysse 80 jours (couvert souple)	12,95 $
(couvert rigide)	16,95 $
□ Journal de voyage Ulysse (spirale)	11,95 $
□ Journal de voyage Ulysse (format poche, bleu)	7,95 $
(format poche, rose)	7,95 $

QUANTITÉ	TITRE	PRIX	TOTAL
		Total partiel	
		Poste-Canada*	4,00 $
		Total partiel	
		T.P.S. 7%	
		Total	

Nom : ....

Adresse : ....

....

....

Paiement :   □ Visa   □ Master Card

Numéro de carte : ....

Expiration : ....   Signature : ....

ULYSSE L'ÉDITEUR DU VOYAGE
4176, rue Saint-Denis, Montréal, Québec
☎ (514) 843-9447 fax (514) 843-9448
Pour l'Europe, s'adresser aux distributeurs, voir liste p. 2
* Pour l'étranger, compter 10 $ de frais d'envoi